Primary Source Accounts of the

Revolutionary
War

James M. Deem

MyReportLinks.com Books

an imprint of

Enslow Publishers, Inc.
Box 398, 40 Industrial Road
Berkeley Heights, NJ 07922
USA

MyReportLinks.com Books, an imprint of Enslow Publishers, Inc. MyReportLinks®
is a registered trademark of Enslow Publishers, Inc.

Library of Congress Cataloging-in-Publication Data

Deem, James M.
  Primary source accounts of the revolutionary war / James M. Deem.
    p. cm. — (America's wars through primary sources)
  Includes bibliographical references and index.
  ISBN-10: 1-59845-004-2
  1. United States—History—Revolution, 1775–1783—Sources—Juvenile literature. I. Title. II. Series.
  E208.D45 2006
  973.3—dc22

                                        2005030044
  ISBN-13: 978-1-59845-004-0

Printed in the United States of America

10 9 8 7 6 5 4 3 2

To Our Readers:
Through the purchase of this book, you and your library gain access to the Report Links that specifically
back up this book.
The Publisher will provide access to the Report Links that back up this book and will keep these Report
Links up to date on **www.myreportlinks.com** for five years from the book's first publication date.
We have done our best to make sure all Internet addresses in this book were active and appropriate when
we went to press. However, the author and the Publisher have no control over, and assume no liability
for, the material available on those Internet sites or on other Web sites they may link to.
The usage of the MyReportLinks.com Books Web site is subject to the terms and conditions stated on the
Usage Policy Statement on **www.myreportlinks.com.**
A password may be required to access the Report Links that back up this book. The password is found
on the bottom of page 4 of this book.
Any comments or suggestions can be sent by e-mail to comments@myreportlinks.com or to the address
on the back cover.

Photo Credits: America's Homepage, p. 14; Bloomsburg University Archives, p. 70; Contemplator.com,
p. 101; Enslow Publishers, Inc., pp. 8, 12; *George Washington Resigning His Commission* by John Trumbull,
1817, U.S. Capitol Rotunda, Architect of the Capitol, p. 113; Gilder Lehrman Institute of American History,
p. 82; Herbert Hoover Presidential Library and Museum, p. 27; History Matters, p. 63; John Singleton
Copley, American, 1738–1815, *Paul Revere*, 1768, Oil on canvas, Museum of Fine Arts, Boston, Gift of
Joseph W. Revere, William B. Revere and Edward H. R. Revere 30.781, p. 10; Library of Congress, pp. 1, 3,
7, 9, 19, 22, 26, 31, 37, 38, 46, 51, 53, 57, 67, 72, 81, 86, 91, 94, 103, 105, 111; Massachusetts Historical
Society, p. 11; Michigan State University, p. 65; MyReportLinks.com Books, p. 4; National Archives and
Records Administration, pp. 17, 29, 35, 55, 59, 61, 78, 109; National Park Service, p. 41; PBS, pp. 75, 89;
Pennsylvania State Archives, p. 93; *Signing of the First Peace Treaty with Great Britain*, Constantino Brumidi,
oil on canvas, ca. 1874, U.S. Senate Collection, p. 107; Smithsonian Institution, pp. 25, 97; United States
Military Academy, p. 44; University of Michigan, Clements Library, p. 36; University of Northern Iowa, p. 33;
University of Virginia, p. 49; Veterans Museum and Memorial Center, p. 84.

Cover Photo: General George Washington and the Marquis de Lafayette at Valley Forge, Pennsylvania,
Library of Congress.

Every effort has been made to locate all copyright holders of material used in this book. If any errors or
omissions have occurred, please contact us at www.myreportlinks.com. We will try to make corrections
in future editions.

CONTENTS

MyReportLinks.com Books
Great Books, Great Links, Great for Research!

The Internet sites featured in this book can save you hours of research time. These Internet sites—we call them **"Report Links"**—are constantly changing, but we keep them up to date on our Web site.

When you see this "Approved Web Site" logo, you will know that we are directing you to a great Internet site that will help you with your research.

Give it a try! Type http://www.myreportlinks.com into your browser, click on the series title and enter the password, then click on the book title, and scroll down to the Report Links listed for this book.

The Report Links will bring you to great source documents, photographs, and illustrations. MyReportLinks.com Books save you time, feature Report Links that are kept up to date, and make report writing easier than ever! A complete listing of the Report Links can be found on pages 114–115 at the back of the book.

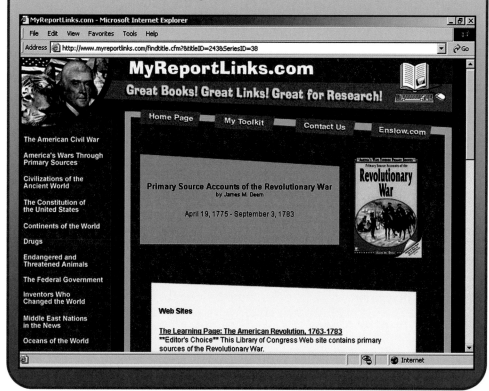

Please see "To Our Readers" on the copyright page for important information about this book, the MyReportLinks.com Web site, and the Report Links that back up this book.

Please enter **PRW2643** if asked for a password.

WHAT ARE PRIMARY SOURCES?

Valley Forge, Pennsylvania

December 14.—. . . I am Sick—discontented—and out of humor. Poor food—hard lodging —Cold Weather—fatigue—Nasty Cloaths—nasty Cookery—Vomit half my time—. . . I can't Endure it—Why are we sent here to starve and Freeze—

—Albigence Waldo, in a journal, December 1777.

The young soldier who wrote these words in his journal never dreamed that they would be read by anyone. They were not intended to be read as a history of the Revolutionary War. But his words—and the words of others that have come down to us through scholars or were saved over generations by family members—are unique resources. Historians call such writings primary source documents. As you read this book, you will find other primary source accounts of the war written by the men and women who fought it. Their letters home reflect their thoughts, their dreams, their fears, and their longing for loved ones. Some of them speak of the excitement of battle, while others mention the everyday boredom of day-to-day life in camp.

But the story of a war is not only the story of the men and women in service. This book also contains diary entries, newspaper accounts, official documents, speeches, and songs of the war years. They reflect the opinions of those who were not in battle but who were still affected by the war. All of these things as well as photographs and art are primary sources—they were created by people who participated in, witnessed, or were affected by the events of the time.

Many of these sources, such as letters and diaries, are a reflection of personal experience. Others, such as newspaper accounts, reflect the mood of the time as well as the opinions of the papers' editors. All of them give us a unique insight into history as it happened. But it is also important to keep in mind that each source reflects its author's biases, beliefs, and background. Each is still someone's interpretation of an event.

Some of the primary sources in this book will be easy to understand; others may not. Their authors came from a different time and were products of different backgrounds and levels of education. So as you read their words, you will see that some of those words may be spelled differently than we would spell them. And some of their stories may be written without the kinds of punctuation we are used to seeing. Each source has been presented as it was originally written, but wherever a word or phrase is unclear or might be misunderstood, an explanation has been added.

TIME LINE OF THE REVOLUTIONARY WAR

1764—Sugar Act.

1765—Stamp Act.

—Quartering Act.

1767—Townshend Revenue Act.

1770—MARCH 5: Boston Massacre.

1773—DECEMBER 16: Boston Tea Party.

1774—SEPTEMBER 5: First Continental Congress meets.

1775—APRIL 19: Battle of Lexington and Concord, Massachusetts.

—JUNE 17: Battle of Bunker Hill (Breed's Hill).

—DECEMBER 31: Battle of Quebec.

1776—JUNE 28: Attack on Charleston, South Carolina.

—JULY 4: Declaration of Independence is adopted by Congress.

—AUGUST 27: Battle of Long Island.

—OCTOBER 28: Battle of White Plains, New York.

—DECEMBER 25–26: Battle of Trenton, New Jersey.

1777—JANUARY 3–4: Battle of Princeton, New Jersey.

—AUGUST 16: Battle of Bennington, New York.

—SEPTEMBER 11: Battle of Brandywine, Pennsylvania.

—SEPTEMBER 19: First battle of Saratoga (Freeman's Farm), New York.

—OCTOBER 4: Battle of Germantown, Pennsylvania.

—OCTOBER 7: Second battle of Saratoga (Bemis Heights), New York.

1778—FEBRUARY 6: French-American treaty of alliance signed.

—JUNE 28: Battle of Monmouth, New Jersey.

—DECEMBER 29: British capture Savannah, Georgia.

1779—JUNE 21: Spain declares war on Britain.

—SEPTEMBER–OCTOBER: Siege of Savannah, Georgia.

1780—MARCH 14: Spanish capture Mobile, Florida.

—MAY 12: British capture Charleston, South Carolina.

—AUGUST 16: Battle of Camden, South Carolina.

—OCTOBER 7: Battle of Kings Mountain, South Carolina.

1781—JANUARY 17: Battle of Hannah's Cowpens, South Carolina.

—MARCH 15: Battle of Guildford Court House, North Carolina.

—MAY 9: Spanish capture Pensacola, Florida.

—SEPTEMBER 28–OCTOBER 19: Battle of Yorktown.

1783—SEPTEMBER 3: Treaty of Paris signed.

—NOVEMBER 25: British leave New York City.

Paul Revere's depiction of the Boston Massacre.

Major Battles of the Revolutionary War

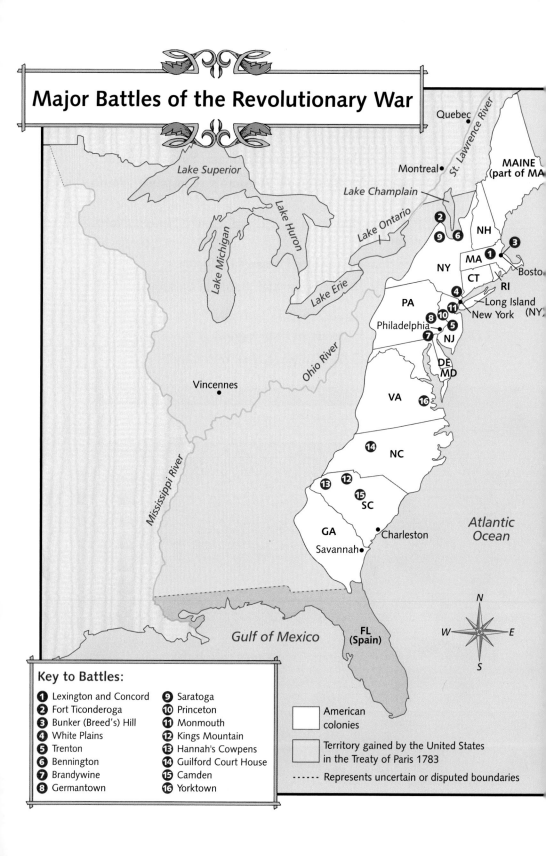

Quebec

St. Lawrence River

Lake Superior

Montreal

Lake Champlain

MAINE (part of MA

Lake Ontario

Lake Huron

Lake Michigan

Lake Erie

NH

MA ❶

❷

❾ ❻

NY

CT

RI

❹

Long Island

New York (NY)

Boston

PA

❽ ❿ ⓫

Philadelphia

❼

❺

NJ

DE
MD

Ohio River

Vincennes

VA ⓰

Mississippi River

⓮ NC

⓭ ⓬

⓯

SC

GA

Charleston

Savannah

Atlantic Ocean

Gulf of Mexico

FL
(Spain)

N

W   E

S

Key to Battles:

❶ Lexington and Concord
❷ Fort Ticonderoga
❸ Bunker (Breed's) Hill
❹ White Plains
❺ Trenton
❻ Bennington
❼ Brandywine
❽ Germantown
❾ Saratoga
❿ Princeton
⓫ Monmouth
⓬ Kings Mountain
⓭ Hannah's Cowpens
⓮ Guilford Court House
⓯ Camden
⓰ Yorktown

American colonies

Territory gained by the United States in the Treaty of Paris 1783

----- Represents uncertain or disputed boundaries

"THE SHOT HEARD ROUND THE WORLD"

By the rude bridge that arched the flood,
Their flag to April's breeze unfurled,
Here once the embattled farmers stood,
And fired the shot heard round the world.

These lines from "The Concord Hymn" by poet
Ralph Waldo Emerson immortalize the first battle in

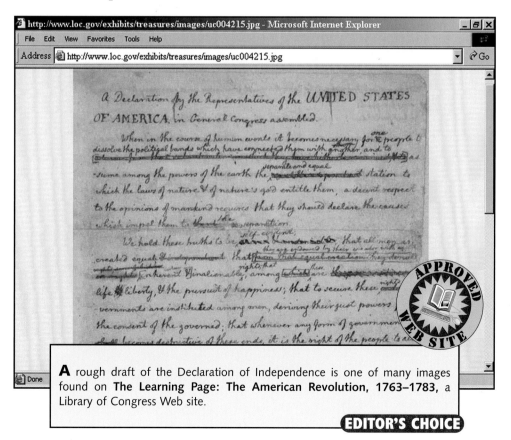

A rough draft of the Declaration of Independence is one of many images
found on **The Learning Page: The American Revolution, 1763–1783**, a
Library of Congress Web site.

EDITOR'S CHOICE

America's war for independence from Great Britain. On April 19, 1775, the "shot heard round the world" came from the muskets of American militiamen firing at British troops on Concord's North Bridge, in eastern Massachusetts. The earlier battle at Lexington, along with the fighting at Concord, marked the beginning of the war between Great Britain and its American colonies known as the Revolutionary War. It was a war fought to secure the rights to "Life, Liberty, and the pursuit of Happiness"

Photograph © 2006 Museum of Fine Arts, Boston.

△ *John Singleton Copley, one of Colonial America's most prominent artists, painted this portrait of Paul Revere, silversmith, in 1768.*

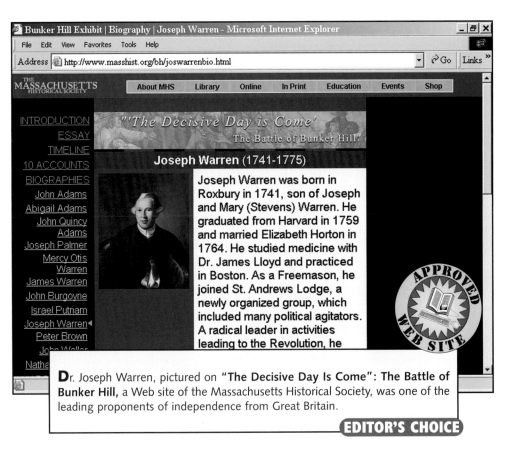

Bunker Hill Exhibit | Biography | Joseph Warren - Microsoft Internet Explorer

File Edit View Favorites Tools Help

Address http://www.masshist.org/bh/joswarrenbio.html Go Links

THE MASSACHUSETTS HISTORICAL SOCIETY

About MHS   Library   Online   In Print   Education   Events   Shop

INTRODUCTION
ESSAY
TIMELINE
10 ACCOUNTS
BIOGRAPHIES
John Adams
Abigail Adams
John Quincy
Adams
Joseph Palmer
Mercy Otis
Warren
James Warren
John Burgoyne
Israel Putnam
Joseph Warren◄
Peter Brown
John Waller
Nathe

"'The Decisive Day is Come'
The Battle of Bunker Hill"

Joseph Warren (1741-1775)

Joseph Warren was born in Roxbury in 1741, son of Joseph and Mary (Stevens) Warren. He graduated from Harvard in 1759 and married Elizabeth Horton in 1764. He studied medicine with Dr. James Lloyd and practiced in Boston. As a Freemason, he joined St. Andrews Lodge, a newly organized group, which included many political agitators. A radical leader in activities leading to the Revolution, he

APPROVED WEB SITE

Dr. Joseph Warren, pictured on **"The Decisive Day Is Come": The Battle of Bunker Hill,** a Web site of the Massachusetts Historical Society, was one of the leading proponents of independence from Great Britain.

EDITOR'S CHOICE

that America's Declaration of Independence would later declare to be the rights of all men.

It was also a war that would last for six and a half years on American soil and eventually involve some of the most powerful nations of Europe before peace was declared in 1783. And it started with farmers and other citizen-soldiers armed with their own weapons in a small Massachusetts town.

▶ Stopping the Rebels

On the night of April 18, 1775, British troops stationed in Boston were ordered to prepare to march.

Their destination was Concord, a town sixteen miles away. The British had learned that rebellious American colonists had a hidden store, or stockpile, of weapons, ammunition, and other supplies there. Two leading rebels, Samuel Adams and John Hancock, were also staying in nearby Lexington, and some historians believe that the British had been ordered to arrest them.

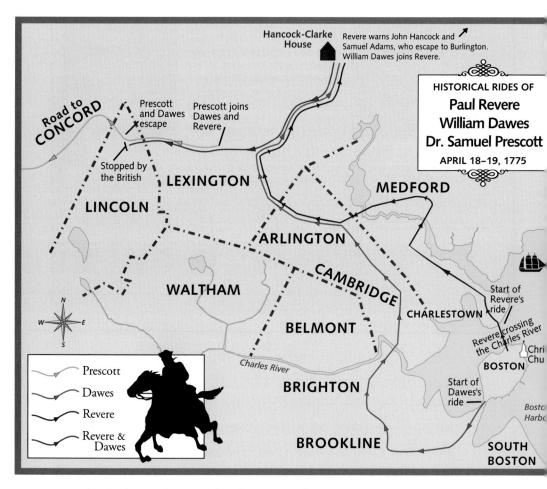

Hancock-Clarke House

Revere warns John Hancock and Samuel Adams, who escape to Burlington. William Dawes joins Revere.

HISTORICAL RIDES OF
Paul Revere
William Dawes
Dr. Samuel Prescott

APRIL 18–19, 1775

Road to CONCORD

Prescott and Dawes escape

Prescott joins Dawes and Revere

Stopped by the British

LEXINGTON

MEDFORD

LINCOLN

ARLINGTON

CAMBRIDGE

WALTHAM

Start of Revere's ride

CHARLESTOWN

BELMONT

Revere crossing the Charles River

Charles River

Chri Chu

BOSTON

Start of Dawes's ride

BRIGHTON

Bosto Harbo

Prescott

Dawes

Revere

Revere & Dawes

BROOKLINE

SOUTH BOSTON

▲ The historical routes of Paul Revere, William Dawes, and Samuel Prescott are traced on this map. Dawes, on the same mission as Revere, left earlier but traveled a longer route to Lexington.

Paul Revere was a Boston silversmith who had become involved in the growing anger of American colonists for the way Great Britain was treating its American colonies. A member of an anti-British organization known as the Sons of Liberty, Revere also acted as a courier. He was asked by Dr. Joseph Warren to ride from Boston to Lexington to warn Samuel Adams and John Hancock that British troops were on their way to seize the store of munitions. Although Revere galloped ahead of the marching British soldiers, the area between Boston and Lexington had many British patrols. As Revere himself testified about his famous ride:

> I set off . . . about 11 oClock, the Moon shone bright. I had got almost over Charlestown Common, towards Cambridge, when I saw two Officers on Horseback, standing under the shade of a Tree, in a narrow part of the roade. . . . One of them Started his horse towards me, the other up the road, as I supposed, to head me should I escape the first. I turned my horse short about, and rid upon a full Gallop for Mistick Road, he followed me about 300 yardes, and finding he could not catch me, returned. I proceeded to Lexington . . . and alarmed Mr Adams & Col. Hancock.[1]

Revere was met by William Dawes, a rider on the same mission who had taken a different route. Continuing toward Concord, they were joined by Dr. Samuel Prescott when soon all three were stopped by British soldiers who threatened Revere, "If you go an Inch further, you are a dead Man."[2]

But Revere was not going to stop.

> [W]e attempted to git thro them, but they kept before us, and swore if we did not turn in to that pasture, they would blow our brains out. . . . they forced us in, when we had got in, Mr Prescot . . . took to the left, I to the right, towards a Wood, at the bottom of the Pasture, intending, when I gained that, to jump my Horse & run afoot; just as I reached it, out started six officers, siesed [seized] my bridle, put their pistols to my Breast, ordered me to dismount, which I did.[3]

When questioned by the commanding officer, Revere identified himself but lied about what he had seen. He reported that British troops had run aground in their attempts to leave Boston and that

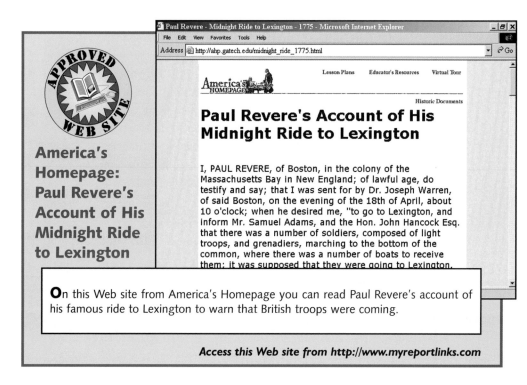

America's
Homepage:
Paul Revere's
Account of His
Midnight Ride
to Lexington

Paul Revere's Account of His Midnight Ride to Lexington

I, PAUL REVERE, of Boston, in the colony of the Massachusetts Bay in New England; of lawful age, do testify and say; that I was sent for by Dr. Joseph Warren, of said Boston, on the evening of the 18th of April, about 10 o'clock; when he desired me, "to go to Lexington, and inform Mr. Samuel Adams, and the Hon. John Hancock Esq. that there was a number of soldiers, composed of light troops, and grenadiers, marching to the bottom of the common, where there was a number of boats to receive them; it was supposed that they were going to Lexington.

On this Web site from America's Homepage you can read Paul Revere's account of his famous ride to Lexington to warn that British troops were coming.

Access this Web site from http://www.myreportlinks.com

he had managed to alert over five hundred rebels who would be arriving soon. Although he was threatened with death a number of times, he was eventually released near Lexington.

Sounding the Alarm in Lexington

Some seventy men who were members of the Massachusetts militia, an informal army of colonists, were stationed on the green behind the town's meetinghouse when Paul Revere arrived at Lexington on the morning of April 19. One of the militiamen was nineteen-year-old Sylvanus Wood. He had heard the general alarm of a ringing bell and hurried to the town.

> When I arrived there, I inquired of Captain [John] Parker, the commander of the Lexington company, what was the news. . . . [W]hile we were talking, a messenger came up and told the captain that the British troops were within half a mile.
>
> Parker led those of us who were equipped to the north end of Lexington Common, near the Bedford road, and formed us in single file. . . . While we were standing, I . . . counted every man who was paraded, and the whole number was thirty-eight. . . .[4]

At about the same time, Revere walked through militiamen assembled on the green. He heard the commanding officer tell the men not to fire on the British troops who were marching into town.

One young British officer, William Sutherland, reported what happened as the British marched into Lexington. A colonist had taken aim at him, but his gun misfired. Sutherland did not attempt to shoot back at the man, simply reporting the event to his commanding officer, Major John Pitcairn. Sutherland described what happened as they continued toward Lexington.

When we came up to the main body [of colonists], which appeared to me to exceed 400 . . . who were drawn up in a plain opposite to the Church, several [British] officers called out, "Throw down your arms, and you shall come to no harm," or words to that effect.[5]

But the Massachusetts militiamen did not disperse, and British soldiers on horseback, among them Sutherland, rode onto the green.

"The Shot Heard Round the World"

As the colonists and the British troops faced each other, a shot rang out. Paul Revere described what happened next.

I heard the report [of the gun], turned my head, and saw the smoake in front of the [British] Troops, they imeaditly gave a great shout, ran a few paces, and then the whole fired. I could first distinguish Iregular fireing, which I suppose was the advance Guard, and then platoons. At the time I could not see our Militia,

No A.   Lexington April 25th, 1775.

I John Parker, of lawful Age, and Commander of the Militia in Lexington, do testify & declare that on the 19th Instant, in the Morning, about one of the Clock, being informed that there were a Number of Regular Officers riding up and down the Road, stopping and insulting People as they passed the Road, and also was informed that a Number of Regular Troops were on their March from Boston, in order to take the Province Stores at Concord, ordered our Militia to meet on the Common in said Lexington, to consult what to do, and concluded not to be discovered, nor meddle or make with said Regular Troops (if they should approach) unless they should insult or molest us — and upon their sudden Approach I immediately ordered our Militia to disperse and not to fire — Immediately said Troops made their Appearance and rushed furiously, fired upon and killed eight of our Party, without receiving any Provocation therefor from us.

John Parker

Middlesex ss. April 25, 1775. The above named John Parker personally appeared, and, after being duly cautioned to declare the whole Truth, made solemn Oath to the Truth of the above Deposition by him subscribed   Coram   Wm Reed
                                Josiah Johnson } Jus of Peace.
                                Wm Stickney

Captain John Parker's deposition, or account, of the battle at Lexington.

for they were covered from me, by a house at the bottom of the Street.[6]

Who fired that first shot? According to British soldier William Sutherland, it was the Americans.

I heard Major Pitcairn's voice call out, "Soldiers, don't fire, keep your ranks, form and surround them." Instantly some of the villains [the colonists] who got over the hedge fired at us which our men for the first time returned, which set my horse a-going who galloped with me down a road above 600 yards, among the middle of them before I turned him. In returning, a vast number who were in a wood . . . fired at me, but the distance was so great that I only heard the Whistling of the Balls, but saw a great number of people in the wood.[7]

Militiaman Sylvanus Wood had another version of the events. As he stood on Lexington Green, he reported that he saw Major John Pitcairn approach the American militia. According to Wood, the British officer

. . . swung his sword, and said, "Lay down your arms, you damned rebels, or you are all dead men—Fire!" Some guns were fired by the British at us from the first platoon, but no person was killed or hurt, being probably charged only with powder.

Just at this time, Captain Parker ordered every man to take care of himself. The company immediately dispersed; and while the company was dispersing and leaping over the wall, the second platoon of the British

fired, and killed some of our men. There was not a gun fired by any of Captain Parker's company, within my knowledge. I was so situated that I must have known it, had anything of the kind taken place before a total dispersion of our company.[8]

Whoever fired first, the shooting continued for about fifteen minutes. When it was over, eight Americans had been killed and ten wounded. Only one British soldier had been wounded.[9]

Heading for Concord

A short time later, as the British troops continued their march toward Concord to destroy the hidden stores of equipment and goods, Sylvanus Wood described what he did.

The Library of Congress: Today in History: April 19

On April 19, 1775, the Revolutionary War began with the Battle of Lexington and Concord. This Web site from the Library of Congress describes the fighting and also discusses the history of the popular war song "Yankee Doodle."

Access this Web site from http://www.myreportlinks.com

> [I] helped carry six dead into the meetinghouse [in
> Lexington] and then set out after the enemy and
> had not an armed man to go with me, but before I
> arrived at Concord I see one of the [British] grenadiers
> [infantry soldiers] standing sentinel [guard]. I cocked
> my piece and run up to him, seized his gun with
> my left hand. He surrendered. . . . This was the first
> prisoner that was known to be taken that day.[10]

At Concord, the British destroyed what stores
were left, including shovels for digging trenches
and food to feed the militia. The citizens of Concord
had already removed most of the stockpile. Corporal
Amos Barrett, a twenty-three-year-old Massachusetts
militiaman, recalled what the British troops did:

> [T]he British came . . . to destroy our stores that we had
> got laid up for our army. There was in the Town House
> a number of entrenching tools which they carried out
> and burnt them. At last they said it was better to burn
> the house, and set fire to them in the house—but our
> people begged . . . them not to burn the house, and put
> it out. It wan't long before it was set fire again. . . .[11]

As the American militiamen began marching
toward the North Bridge, they saw flames coming
from Concord and thought that the British were
trying to burn the town. When the British troops
guarding the bridge saw the Americans approach-
ing, they began pulling up planks to prevent the

militia from crossing. American Amos Barrett described the scene as the British fired three warning shots at the colonists:

> We then saw the whole body [of British troops] a-coming out of town. We then was ordered to lay behind a wall that run over a hill, and when they got nigh enough, Major Buttrick said he would give the word "fire," but they did not come quite so near as he expected before they halted. . . . If we had fired, I believe that we could have killed almost every officer there was in the front. . . .[12]

Back to Boston

The situation changed as the British retreated to Boston. As Barrett recalled, "We was soon after them . . . and a great many killed. When I got there, a great many lay dead and the road was bloody."[13]

British sources depict the march back to Boston more vividly. British lieutenant John Barker wrote that no sooner had the troops marched a half-mile from Lexington than shots rang out.

> We were fired on from houses and behind trees, and before we had gone one-half mile we were fired on from all sides, but mostly from the rear. . . . In this way we marched between nine and ten miles, their numbers increasing from all parts, while ours was reducing by deaths, wounds and fatigue. . . .[14]

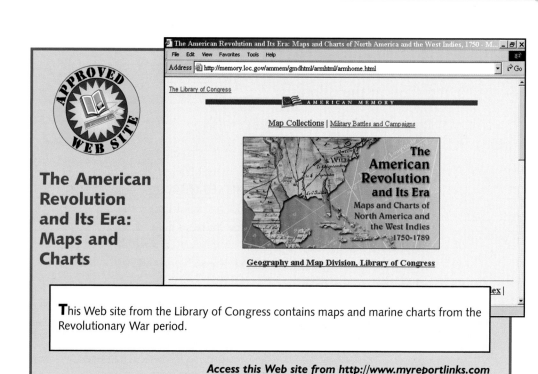

The American Revolution and Its Era: Maps and Charts

This Web site from the Library of Congress contains maps and marine charts from the Revolutionary War period.

Access this Web site from http://www.myreportlinks.com

British lieutenant Frederick Mackenzie recorded his experiences of the day in a diary.

Many of [the Rebels] were killed in the houses on the road side from whence they fired; in some of them 7 or 8 men were destroyed. . . . If we had had time to set fire to those houses many Rebels must have perished in them. . . .[15]

Peter Oliver, although a Bostonian by birth, was a Loyalist. He, like nearly one third of all American colonists, was sympathetic toward Great Britain. Oliver described the bravery of the British soldiers as they fought a well-hidden force of rebels on the way back to Boston:

> Many were the Instances of the british Soldiers great Humanity, in protecting the aged, the Women & the Children from Injury; . . . A Soldier seeing an old Man, with a Musket, who had been in the Battle, much wounded & leaning against a Wall; he went up to him, tore off the Lining of his own Coat & bound up his Wounds, with it, desiring him to go out of Harm's Way. The Soldier had scarcely turned from him, when the old Man fired at his deliverer: human Passion could not bear such Ingratitude, & the Man lost his Life by it.[16]

Oliver also wrote about the exploits of a daring American woman whose refusal to lay down her guns led to her death.

> There was a remarkable Heroine, who stood at an House Door firing at the Kings Troops; there being Men within who loaded Guns for her to fire. She was desired to withdraw, but she answered, only by Insults from her own Mouth, & by Balls from the Mouths of her Muskets. This brought on her own Death, & the Deaths of those who were within Doors.[17]

▶ A Heavy Toll

The British troops marched back into Boston, having suffered casualties. British lieutenant Frederick Mackenzie kept a record of the number of British dead and wounded on that day in April 1775. The list did not include officers, so the casualties were even higher.

Return of the Killed, Wounded, & Missing in the Action of the 19th April 1775.

Corps.	Killed.	Wd.	Missing
4th	7 –	25 –	8
5th	5 –	15 –	1
10th	1 –	13 –	1
18th	1 –	4 –	1
23rd	4 –	26 –	6
38th	4 –	12 –	
43rd	4 –	5 –	2
47th	5 –	22 –	
52nd	3 –	2 –	1
59th	3 –	3 –	
Marines	31 –	38 –	2
Artillery	–	2 –	
Total	68 –	167 –	22

Officers Not Included.[18]

The number of Americans wounded and killed at Lexington and Concord is not known for certain, although historians generally estimate the total at about one hundred.

A Commander Is Chosen

The fighting of April 19, 1775, was just the beginning of a long and bloody war between Great Britain and its American colonies. Two months later, a Virginian named George Washington, a veteran of the

French and Indian War, was unanimously selected by the Continental Congress to train and command a diverse and disorganized group of men into the first regular army of the colonies. Called the Continental Force, it was later renamed the Continental Army, and Washington requested no salary to lead it. In a letter to Burwell Bassett, the nephew of his wife, George Washington confided his reluctance to take on such a monumental task.

I am now Imbarkd on a tempestuous Ocean from whence, perhaps, no friendly harbour is to be found.

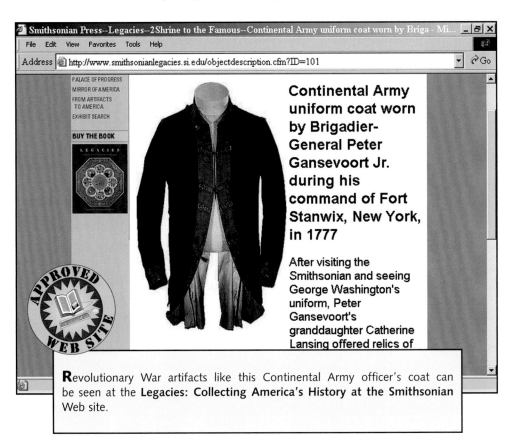

Revolutionary War artifacts like this Continental Army officer's coat can be seen at the **Legacies: Collecting America's History at the Smithsonian** Web site.

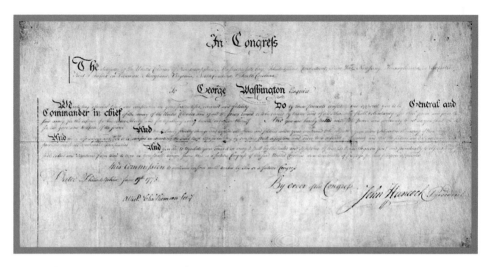

On June 19, 1775, the Continental Congress commissioned George Washington "commander-in-chief of the army of the United Colonies." Washington knew the task he was about to take on would be difficult, describing it as an "honour I by no means aspired to."

I have been called upon by the unanimous Voice of the Colonies to the Command of the Continental Army— It is an honour I by no means aspired to—It is an honour I wished to avoid. . . .[19]

Despite his reluctance—and the overwhelming odds against a small colonial force defeating a great military power—there would be no turning back for Washington or the colonies. The Revolutionary War had begun.

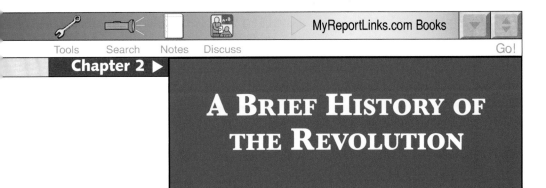
A BRIEF HISTORY OF THE REVOLUTION

By 1763, with the British defeat of the French in the French and Indian War, Great Britain controlled Canada and the continent east of the Mississippi River in North America. With that victory, though, Great Britain had also accumulated a massive debt. The most powerful nation in the world, its resources

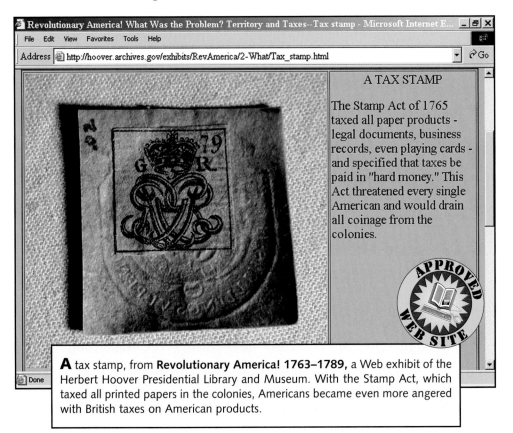

Revolutionary America! What Was the Problem? Territory and Taxes--Tax stamp - Microsoft Internet E...

File   Edit   View   Favorites   Tools   Help

Address   http://hoover.archives.gov/exhibits/RevAmerica/2-What/Tax_stamp.html   Go

A TAX STAMP

The Stamp Act of 1765 taxed all paper products - legal documents, business records, even playing cards - and specified that taxes be paid in "hard money." This Act threatened every single American and would drain all coinage from the colonies.

Done

APPROVED WEB SITE

A tax stamp, from **Revolutionary America! 1763–1789,** a Web exhibit of the Herbert Hoover Presidential Library and Museum. With the Stamp Act, which taxed all printed papers in the colonies, Americans became even more angered with British taxes on American products.

were stretched thin. To make sure that the American colonies were well protected, the British government decided to station regular troops there on a permanent basis. Great Britain also decided to make the American colonies pay for this protection through taxation.

Taxes and the Sons of Liberty

A series of taxes were imposed on the American colonies in the first two years after the French and Indian War. The first group of taxes, known as the Sugar Act, were passed in 1764. The second, the Stamp Act, came in 1765.

The Sugar Act imposed a three-cent tax on each gallon of any non-British sugar imported to the colonies, but the act also collected additional taxes on coffee, wine, silk, and other fabrics. The Stamp Act created a tax on all printed papers, including playing cards and newspapers. Both acts angered the colonists, who believed that they were being taxed unfairly.

When the Stamp Act was passed, many Americans decided to band together to work against the taxes. Begun in Boston in the summer of 1765, the Sons of Liberty was an organization of printers, publishers, shopkeepers, and other workers who protested the taxes. By the end of 1765, this group had members in all thirteen colonies.

Other acts enraged the colonists. These included the Quartering Act of 1765 and the Townshend

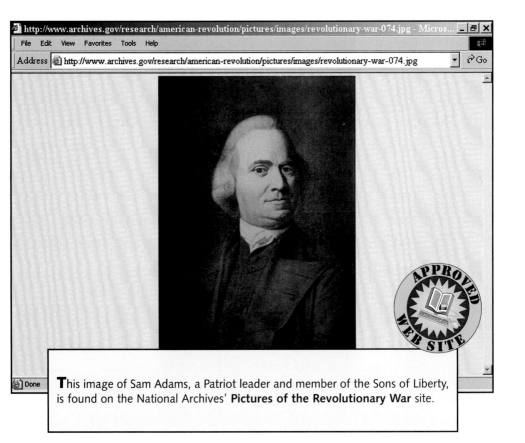

http://www.archives.gov/research/american-revolution/pictures/images/revolutionary-war-074.jpg - Micros...

File   Edit   View   Favorites   Tools   Help

Address   http://www.archives.gov/research/american-revolution/pictures/images/revolutionary-war-074.jpg   Go

Done

This image of Sam Adams, a Patriot leader and member of the Sons of Liberty, is found on the National Archives' **Pictures of the Revolutionary War** site.

Revenue Act of 1767. The Quartering Act required the colonies to provide free housing for British soldiers in inns, public houses, or unoccupied buildings. The Townshend Act added customs duties on imported goods such as paper, oil, glass, paint, lead, and tea. These acts created even more anger among the colonists toward Great Britain, and tensions rose.

The Boston Massacre

To maintain order, the British government sent four thousand British troops to Boston, where citizens were particularly unhappy. Most Bostonians resented the British troops, and many stories, often untrue, circulated about the British.

On the evening of March 5, 1770, what has become known as the Boston Massacre took place. Some boys playing outside the customs house began to taunt a British guard with snowballs. Other soldiers came to his aid, but a large group began to form outside the customs house and confronted the outnumbered soldiers. The frightened troops ordered the mob to break up, but angry citizens remained where they were. British troops then fired into the crowd, killing three colonists immediately. Among them was Crispus Attucks, a black seaman who had been a slave. Two other colonists died of their wounds, and five others were wounded.

This confrontation between British troops and American colonists was used by the Sons of Liberty and others to further the cause of independence from Great Britain. Paul Revere created an engraving of the massacre that showed British soldiers killing American colonists. Its depiction was inaccurate and exaggerated, which served its purpose as Patriot propaganda.[1] It made Americans who were already angry with the British even angrier. British troops were removed from Boston as a result.

▷ The Boston Tea Party

Although the duties, or taxes, imposed by the Townshend Act were eventually repealed, the duty on tea was retained. Many colonists refused to purchase

Boston Massacre - Microsoft Internet Explorer

File   Edit   View   Favorites   Tools   Help

Address http://www.americaslibrary.gov/jb/revolut/jb_revolut_boston_1_e.html

Done

Paul Revere's engraving of the **Boston Massacre** stirred up patriotic fervor among colonists who already disliked British troops stationed in Massachusetts. Learn more about the event and its portrayal by Revere at this Library of Congress site.

tea from Great Britain and instead smuggled it in from other countries. Great Britain's East India Tea Company ended up with a great deal of unsold tea and nearly went bankrupt.

To improve the situation, the British government decided to help the East India Tea Company by passing the Tea Act of 1773. Although this act added an additional tax on tea, it actually made British tea less expensive than smuggled tea. But the colonists still refused to purchase any British tea.

When the *Dartmouth,* a ship loaded with tea, sailed into Boston Harbor on November 28, 1773, colonists led by Samuel Adams called for it to sail back to England. Soon, two other ships carrying tea joined the *Dartmouth*. Unruly crowds threatened violence if the ships were unloaded. Although the captain of the *Dartmouth* agreed to return to England, the British authorities in Boston refused to let it leave.

On the night of December 16, 1773, a group of about fifty colonists dressed as Mohawk Indians raided the three ships, split open the chests of tea on board, and dumped the tea into the harbor. This event became known as the Boston Tea Party. Other "tea parties" were staged in New York, Maryland, and New Jersey, as Americans protested the British taxes levied on the colonists and tried to keep Americans from buying any British tea.

▶ The Intolerable Acts

In 1774, the British government reacted to the protests by the colonists by passing even more stern legislation.

With the four Restraining Acts, which England popularly referred to as the Coercive Acts and the American colonists called the Intolerable Acts, the British government had four aims. First, it tried to restore order to Boston by closing its harbor until the East India Tea Company was reimbursed for the tea destroyed by Americans. Second, it gave the British governor of the Massachusetts colony the power to appoint local government officials, such

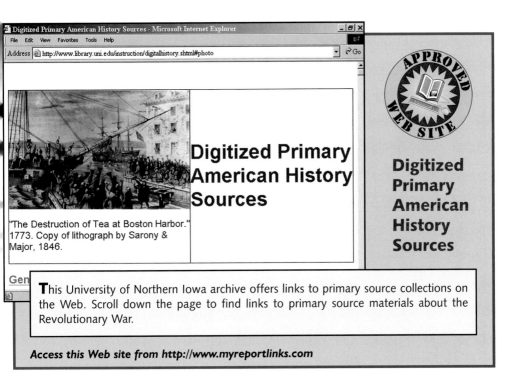

Digitized Primary American History Sources - Microsoft Internet Explorer

File   Edit   View   Favorites   Tools   Help

Address   http://www.library.uni.edu/instruction/digitalhistory.shtml#photo   Go

Digitized Primary American History Sources

"The Destruction of Tea at Boston Harbor."
1773. Copy of lithograph by Sarony &
Major, 1846.

Digitized Primary American History Sources

This University of Northern Iowa archive offers links to primary source collections on the Web. Scroll down the page to find links to primary source materials about the Revolutionary War.

Access this Web site from http://www.myreportlinks.com

as sheriffs, to uphold British law despite colonists' objections, and it limited the power of town meetings. Third, the acts allowed British soldiers and other officials accused of crimes to be tried in England rather than in America. Fourth, in a harsher version of the earlier Quartering Act, British soldiers were to be housed in private homes if public accommodations were not available. While this last act applied to all of the colonies, the Intolerable Acts were mainly intended to punish the city of Boston and the colony of Massachusetts.

Although not part of the Restraining Acts, the Quebec Act was equally intolerable to American colonists. It established a generous boundary for the

French province of Quebec in Canada, which cut into territories that Massachusetts, Connecticut, and Virginia, among other colonies, hoped to develop one day.

▷ The First Continental Congress

Both the Intolerable Acts and the Quebec Act—and the dissatisfaction that they caused—led to the meeting of the First Continental Congress at Carpenter's Hall (later renamed Independence Hall) in Philadelphia on September 5, 1774. All of the thirteen colonies except Georgia sent delegates who met for over a month. This congress did not meet to declare the colonies' independence from Britain, however. Its purpose was to organize and present a united response to the British government's heavy-handed control of the colonies. It did this with a petition, called the Declaration of Rights and Grievances, which it sent to George III, the king of the United Kingdom of Great Britain and Ireland.

The members of Congress also invited the people of Canada to join in their appeal to the king to restore harmony between Great Britain and its North American colonies, but to no avail.

The British government did not respond directly to the meeting of the First Continental Congress, but it increased the number of soldiers stationed in Boston. In turn, the colonists began to stockpile weapons and ammunition that might be necessary if a war began. When they could, British troops

The Continental Congress's petition to George III in 1774 did not threaten rebellion. Its authors considered themselves faithful subjects of the Crown, as the petition's opening lines state.

tracked down these hidden stores and seized them.

Lexington, Concord, and Bunker Hill

By 1775, tensions had ignited in the Massachusetts towns of Lexington and Concord, where British troops and American militiamen clashed. By the time the British troops marched back to Charlestown and were ferried across the harbor to Boston, the Patriots' militia chose not to follow. News of the encounters spread quickly throughout the colonies.

Other towns and colonies, anxious to help the Massachusetts militia, sent their own troops to the Boston area. The fighting at Lexington and Concord signaled the need for a second Continental Congress, which met on May 10, again in Philadelphia. On that same day, a small band of Americans known as the Green Mountain Boys, led by Ethan Allen and Benedict Arnold, captured Fort

An image of George III, the British monarch at the time of the Revolutionary War, can be found on the **Spy Letters of the American Revolution** site.

Ticonderoga in New York State from the small British garrison stationed there. The cannon taken from the fort would eventually be moved to the outskirts of Boston and aimed at the British.

By May 31, perhaps as many as seventeen thousand militiamen converged on the hilly outskirts of Boston, awaiting further orders while British forces were strengthened with more troops and officers. Lieutenant General Thomas Gage, the commanding officer of the British troops as well as the governor of the Massachusetts colony, ordered his men to position themselves on two high points outside of Boston: Dorchester Heights and Charlestown.

When the Americans learned of this plan, they quickly moved to secure Bunker Hill and Breed's Hill, the two highest hills in Charlestown. There on the night of June 16, 1775, American colonel William Prescott ordered his men to dig earthen defenses called redoubts to protect themselves from an assault. Though Breed's Hill was the smaller of the two hills, it was situated closer to Boston Harbor. That made it a perfect spot for setting up cannons aimed at the British ships anchored there.

By morning, the American troops were still working when British lookouts observed them and shot cannonballs their way. Although the artillery did little damage to the fortifications, one militiaman was decapitated and the Americans' only water supply was destroyed. By noon, demoralized by the

▲ *This engraving made in the mid-eighteenth century offers a view of Colonial Boston from the southeast.*

gruesome death of a fellow soldier, lacking water, and faced with no reinforcements of fresh troops, some of the militia began to desert.[2] Colonel Prescott asked his men to remain at their posts, but he was not entirely successful.

At the same time, British warships continued to bombard the American forces while about twenty-five hundred British troops under the command of General William Howe were ferried across the harbor to Charlestown. By one o'clock, they were positioned for an assault.

Although the battle that followed is called the Battle of Bunker Hill, the main fighting took place on Breed's Hill. It was a terrible and bloody confrontation. The British attacked the American redoubts three times. Although the Americans were

▲ The Battle of Bunker Hill is depicted in this nineteenth-century print. The battle, which was actually fought on Breed's Hill, pitted an outmanned group of Colonial fighters against a much larger and better-trained British force.

forced to retreat from their position when their ammunition ran out, the victory cost the British dearly. About 230 British soldiers were killed and over 800 were wounded, almost 45 percent of the British army's force.[3] The Americans lost about 140 men, most of them in the final retreat. There were 271 Americans wounded and 30 captured.

Although the British had taken Breed's Hill, the victory amounted to little. The Americans had proven themselves to be worthy opponents, but the need for a regular well-trained army was evident. On July 2, George Washington arrived in Cambridge, Massachusetts, nominated by John Adams and then unanimously elected by the Second Continental Congress to take command of the army.

The Battle of Quebec

Late in June 1775, the Second Continental Congress ordered an attack on British-held Canada. Brigadier General Benedict Arnold was recruited by General Washington to command eleven hundred men in this mission. Arnold spent August and part of September gathering the necessary men and supplies.

Arnold planned to march from Maine, then part of the Massachusetts colony, to Quebec in twelve days, but using outdated and inaccurate maps, he had underestimated the distance by half. The trip took forty-five days, during which his men faced food shortages and difficult weather conditions. In fact, lack of food became such a problem that some

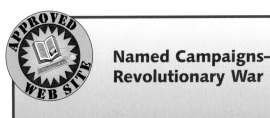

Named Campaigns— Revolutionary War

Access this Web site from http://www.myreportlinks.com

Learn about the named campaigns of the Revolutionary War on this Web site from the United States Army Center of Military History.

of Arnold's men resorted to eating boiled candles, shoe leather, and one of their own dogs. By the time Arnold and his troops arrived at Quebec in mid-November, he had only six hundred men left of the twelve hundred he had begun with. Nearly three hundred had deserted, others had become ill from sleeping in the cold and damp, and still others had died from starvation and sickness.[4]

By the time the battle began in the early morning of December 31, 1775, Arnold's troops had been reinforced and numbered nearly a thousand. Snow fell as the American forces were met with British artillery. Arnold was wounded in the leg and gave up his command to a subordinate officer. Quebec's defenses proved to be solid, and in only three hours, the Americans began to give up.

Sixty Americans were killed in the Battle of Quebec, and more than four hundred others were captured while the British lost only five men, with thirteen wounded. Over the course of the next ten months, the British pushed the American forces back to Fort Ticonderoga on the western shore of Lake Champlain.

The British Leave Boston

By the early part of 1776, many Americans believed that they had been fighting half a war. There had been battles, but no decisive victories had been won on either side. In the meantime, the British remained in Boston out of fear of further attacks. General Washington wanted to engage the British troops in battle, but in March 1776, after the colonists used the artillery captured at Fort Ticonderoga to bombard the city, the British chose to evacuate Boston.

The Assembly Room in Independence Hall restored to 1776. - Microsoft Internet Explorer

File   Edit   View   Favorites   Tools   Help

Address http://www.cr.nps.gov/museum/exhibits/revwar/image_gal/indeimg/assembly.html

The Assembly Room in Independence Hall, then known as the State House. It was in this room that the Second Continental Congress debated severing ties with Great Britain and issued its Declaration of Independence. View more images of this important historical site at the **National Park Service Museum Collections: American Revolutionary War** Web page.

Declaring Independence

As the Second Continental Congress continued to meet, the issue of independence from Great Britain arose. Although many Americans still wanted peace with the British, others, most notably Samuel and John Adams, pushed for independence. Many of the delegates, however, still favored union with Great Britain until Thomas Paine's pamphlet *Common Sense* created a furor.

Paine, an Englishman with no love for the British monarchy, had come to America in 1774. Outraged by the British action at the Battle of Lexington and Concord, he published *Common Sense* in January 1776, and within a few months, more than 500,000 Americans had read it. Soon, its call for the American colonies' independence from Great Britain, a still-radical idea at the time, had convinced even the most conservative members of Congress to break with Great Britain.

In the spring and summer of 1776, the Second Continental Congress considered a resolution for independence. On June 7, Richard Henry Lee, a Virginia delegate, proposed "That these United Colonies are, and of right ought to be, free and independent States."[5] The Congress delayed voting on this resolution until July 2, but asked a committee, which included Thomas Jefferson, Benjamin Franklin, and John Adams, to write a declaration of independence, in case Lee's resolution was approved. The bulk of the writing fell to Jefferson.

Although revisions were made, the members of Congress adopted the Declaration of Independence on July 4, 1776.

▶ The Battles for New York

A few months earlier, General George Washington toured the area around New York City and made decisions about how to defend it from the British. Two forts on the Hudson River were built, but most of the twenty thousand troops that Washington requested were sent to Brooklyn Heights, Long Island, just across the East River from Manhattan Island.

On August 22, 1776, over fourteen thousand British soldiers were ferried from Staten Island to Long Island. A few days later, the number had risen to twenty thousand, and the stage was set for one of the most pivotal battles of the Revolutionary War.

The battle was fought the morning of August 27. At 9 o'clock that morning, two brigades of troops— one British, one Hessian (from Prussia, now Germany)—attacked the American line. The center of the American defenses, however, quickly collapsed, and bloody combat with bayonets took place in the trenches.

By noon, the British had reached Brooklyn Heights. Had they continued their attack, they would have captured New York. But Admiral Richard Howe, the commanding officer of the British fleet in America, assumed that Brooklyn

Heights was better defended by the Americans than it actually was. That gave the Americans time to evacuate their positions, under the order of General Washington. Without the British realizing it, some ninety-five hundred American troops were ferried from Long Island to Manhattan across the East River.

Safely evacuated, Washington could take stock of the defeat on Long Island. Over three thousand Americans had been killed or wounded in the Battle of Long Island, and fifteen hundred others had been taken prisoner by the British. British forces had lost

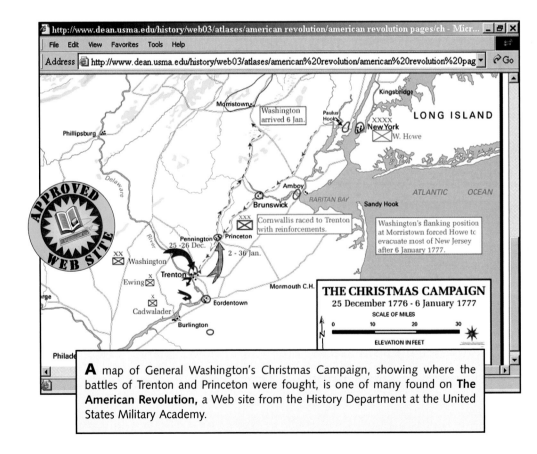

A map of General Washington's Christmas Campaign, showing where the battles of Trenton and Princeton were fought, is one of many found on **The American Revolution,** a Web site from the History Department at the United States Military Academy.

only three hundred men with another five hundred wounded.[6]

Some two weeks later, British troops did cross the East River and began a series of assaults on American forces there. Eventually, General Washington, fearful that his troops might be cut in half, ordered most of his men to march twenty miles north and regroup in White Plains, New York, where they would be able to offer a better defense. The rest of his men were stationed at Fort Washington on the Hudson River.

Washington's plan did not work. On October 28, British troops took White Plains. And on November 16, Fort Washington, besieged by the British, fell quickly and was forced to surrender. Almost three hundred British soldiers were killed, while the Americans lost only fifty-four. But over twenty-eight hundred Americans were taken prisoner that day.

With multiple defeats in New York, the American forces moved into New Jersey.

▷ The Battles of Trenton and Princeton

Admiral Howe followed Washington's troops across New Jersey. By December 8, British forces were stationed in Trenton, and Washington's men had crossed the Delaware River to Pennsylvania. As winter approached, however, British troops were ordered to make winter quarters there. In the meantime, Washington bided his time and regrouped.

On the night of December 25, Washington ordered his men to cross the Delaware during a sleet

A pivotal event in the war, Washington's nighttime crossing of the Delaware River to launch a surprise attack on the Hessians stationed in Trenton, is depicted romantically, if not accurately. Washington would not have been able to stand in the boat without losing his balance.

storm and march five miles to Trenton, while Hessian troops had celebrated Christmas Eve. By 4:00 A.M., Washington's troops had been ferried across the river. At 8:00 A.M. they reached Trenton. The Hessians were caught by surprise, and the battle lasted less than an hour. Only four Americans were wounded, but the Hessians had twenty-two men killed and nearly one thousand were taken prisoner.

The Battle of Princeton

Washington held Trenton, but British forces under the command of Major General Charles Cornwallis were eager to stop the Americans' advance. On January 2, 1777, eight thousand British soldiers cornered Washington and his men on the other side of Assunpink Creek, near Trenton. Cornwallis delayed a final assault against Washington and his men until the following morning. Believing that Washington was trapped, Cornwallis thought the Americans could be easily defeated the next day.

But Washington was a clever general who had no reason to wait for the British attack. Instead, he ordered a few hundred men to make camp with brightly burning fires across from the British. They were ordered to dig and make plenty of noise doing so. But these men were simply a diversion, an attempt to lull Cornwallis into believing that Washington would be an easy mark in the morning.

While the men dug all night, Washington and the majority of his troops left for Princeton on a recently constructed road that the British were unaware of. Not only was Cornwallis surprised, so were the British troops stationed in Princeton. They retreated northeast toward New Brunswick, although some three hundred were captured and perhaps another three hundred killed or wounded. Approximately forty-four Americans died in the battle, including fourteen officers.

His men exhausted, Washington ordered his troops to take up their winter quarters in Morristown. Not many weeks earlier, the British had taken control of New Jersey. Now they were confined to New Brunswick and Amboy, and the Americans were in charge.

The Battles for Philadelphia: Brandywine and Germantown

By spring, Philadelphia had become an important target for the British. Admiral Howe decided to attack the city that symbolized the Colonial revolution itself, and he intended to do so from the sea. When Washington heard that British troops were landing at the northern end of Chesapeake Bay, he positioned his eighteen-thousand-man army at Brandywine Creek, about twenty-five miles southwest in Delaware. They planned to stop the British after an eighteen-mile march from their landing site.

When they clashed on September 11, 1777, British troops were successful in pushing back the American lines. The Americans probably lost more

Papers of George Washington - Microsoft Internet Explorer

File   Edit   View   Favorites   Tools   Help

Address   http://gwpapers.virginia.edu/maps/portraits/trumbull.html

Done

A painting of General Washington by John Trumbull is one of many images of the Revolutionary War hero and first president found on **The Papers of George Washington,** a Web site of the University of Virginia.

than one thousand men that day, though no official figures were recorded. They might have lost many more, if British soldiers had not been so exhausted after their long march.

Over the next few weeks, the armies fought a number of skirmishes, but the British were on their way to Philadelphia. For safety, the Continental Congress had moved to Lancaster, Pennsylvania. On September 26, British troops marched into Philadelphia. The troops were dispersed, but the largest group—over nine thousand—set up camp in

Germantown, five miles northwest of the city. General Washington decided to surprise them.

Washington devised a complex plan of attack. He ordered his men to march twenty miles during the night to reach the outskirts of Germantown. At 5 o'clock in the morning of October 4, he ordered his men to attack, using only their bayonets without firing shots. But a heavy fog and a great deal of confusion hampered the attack. Although the Americans lost the battle, they sensed that they might have won if it had not been for the poor weather.

▷ The Battles for Saratoga

At the same time that the battle for Philadelphia was taking place, British troops were waging a battle on another front. Hoping to divide the colonies in half, so that forces in the New England states would be cut off from those in the Middle Atlantic, the British entered the United States from Canada. Their goal was to take control of the Hudson River.

On July 5 and 6, 1777, ten thousand British troops commanded by Lieutenant General John Burgoyne forced three thousand American troops to abandon Fort Ticonderoga and retreat south. Burgoyne and his troops followed the Americans, but with great difficulty. Under the orders of General Philip Schuyler, American soldiers made the journey for the British extremely difficult. Among other tricks, they cut trees to block the road, destroyed bridges, pushed boulders into a creek to stop any boats, and ran off livestock that might provide food. By slowing the British and making their march so much more difficult, they forced them to travel slowly and consume more of their supplies. It was not long before they faced food shortages.

On August 11, as his army neared Saratoga, New York, Burgoyne ordered six hundred men to Bennington, New Hampshire (now Vermont), to look for supplies. A few days later, he sent another group of soldiers to help them. Both groups were attacked by American forces and soundly defeated. More than one thousand British troops were lost at

British general John Burgoyne's bold plan of invading the United States from Canada succeeded until he reached Saratoga, where he was forced to surrender nearly six thousand men.

Bennington, including over two hundred killed and seven hundred captured.[7]

Without sufficient food and facing a shortage of ammunition, Burgoyne and his troops pushed south past Saratoga. As they did, the Americans reinforced their troops. Now they had seven thousand men, compared to the six thousand that Burgoyne led. All they needed was a place to meet the British in battle.

They chose Bemis Heights, a heavily wooded plateau that rose above the Hudson River. There, in two battles fought eighteen days apart, the Americans decisively defeated the almost-starving British. Many historians agree these victories were largely due to the leadership shown by American general Benedict Arnold. With his retreat blocked, Burgoyne was forced to surrender nearly six thousand men. According to an agreement reached on October 16, the captured British soldiers were to be sent back to England. Fearing that they would be returned to fight the Americans again, the Second Continental Congress made sure that they were located in Virginia for the remainder of the war.

As a result of the defeat of the British at Saratoga, the British were no longer a threat to the Hudson River or to New England.

▷ France and Spain Enter the War

Early in 1778, the United States signed an agreement with France that created an alliance between the two countries. With France on America's side, the war became global, for France could attack Britain anywhere around the world.

As a result, Great Britain changed its strategy. Philadelphia was to be evacuated and troops redeployed through New York to the West Indies. As British troops and many citizens loyal to the king of England left Philadelphia, the Continental Army moved into the city and began to follow the twelve-mile-long retreat column as it marched for Sandy Hook, New Jersey, where the British would be shipped to New York. Ten days later, on June 28, 1778, a battle broke out between the British rear

Persuading the government of France to come to the aid of the American colonists had largely been the work of Benjamin Franklin, pictured at the French court in 1778. **Benjamin Franklin: In His Own Words,** a Library of Congress site, contains this image of Franklin and others.

guard and American forces at Monmouth, New Jersey, that turned out to be the longest battle of the war. Neither side could claim a decisive victory, and British troops reached New York on July 6, 1777.

Not long afterward, French ships arrived with four thousand soldiers, and the Revolutionary War became more complicated. The Battle of Monmouth was the last major battle fought in the northern colonies. The battlefront moved elsewhere. During the fall of 1778, the French and British fought in the West Indies and India, and at the end of December, the British captured Savannah, Georgia.

The war widened when Spain joined forces with the French against the British on May 8, 1779. Their navies even planned an invasion of Great Britain during the summer of 1779. Although they had sixty-six ships and the British Navy was in Ireland and unable to stop an invasion, the invasion never took place.

Later, Spain besieged Gibraltar, and a combined American and Spanish force captured Baton Rouge in the Louisiana Territory. The French attempted to seize Newport, Rhode Island, which the British had held for years. Although the French failed, Britain decided to consolidate its northern forces and move them to New York City and renew its southern campaign.

Battling for the Carolinas

The worst American defeat of the Revolutionary War took place at Charleston, South Carolina, in the spring of 1780. Under siege for more than a month by over seventeen thousand British troops commanded by General Henry Clinton, American general Benjamin Lincoln had no choice but to surrender without a fight. More than a thousand American soldiers were taken prisoner on May 12, 1780.

The Americans met the British in southern battles numerous times as the British set out to control all of the Carolinas, often with brutal tactics at the expense of the colonists.

Colonel Banastre Tarleton's forces were defeated by a combined American force of regular army soldiers, militiamen, and backwoods riflemen at the Battle of Hannah's Cowpens, a frontier pasture, in South Carolina.

One major battle took place at Kings Mountain, in South Carolina, on October 7, 1780. A force of two thousand hardy local volunteers defeated eight hundred British militiamen recruited from Loyalists in the Charleston area. The American victory was a terrible display of vengeance. More than one hundred fifty British soldiers were killed, many after they had surrendered, and some even after they were wounded. Almost seven hundred were taken prisoner, though many later died of their wounds.

Morgan's Masterful Victory

Almost three months later, on January 17, 1781, a second battle took place, nearby at Hannah's Cowpens, a meadow used for cattle. A British force of eleven hundred men led by Lieutenant Colonel Banastre Tarleton was defeated by a combined American force of riflemen, militiamen, and Continental Army soldiers under the command of General Daniel Morgan. Though Tarleton escaped with a few hundred men, one hundred British soldiers were killed in the battle and another eight hundred were taken prisoner, including two hundred men who had been wounded. The Americans also captured eight hundred muskets and almost all of Tarleton's horses and ammunition. The Americans also captured sixty slaves who accompanied the British troops.[8] Congress was so pleased with General Morgan's victory that it voted to award him a gold medal.

▷ Virginia and Yorktown

British forces eventually withdrew from the Carolinas, leaving only small numbers of troops in Charleston and Savannah. By the summer of 1781, almost all British troops from the south were headed for Virginia, where British generals planned to put an end to the rebellion once and for all.

By July, Lieutenant General Charles Cornwallis was ordered to set up a winter camp for the Royal Navy in Yorktown, located southeast of Williamsburg, where the York River meets the Chesapeake Bay.

▲ *Most depictions of Cornwallis's surrender at Yorktown, including this one, show the British general offering his sword to Washington, but the defeated leader sent a subordinate in his place.*

At the same time, General Washington joined forces with French commanders and decided to attack Cornwallis and his troops. Their combined forces of sixteen thousand men reached Yorktown on September 26, 1781, and within a few days had placed it under siege. On October 9, by now well entrenched, the American and French troops began to bombard the British with artillery and gunfire. Needing more men and more supplies that could come only from New York, Cornwallis held out as long as he could.

On October 18, the American and French guns began another attack, but the English had run out of ammunition. Around 9 o'clock that morning, a British drummer boy stood up on the British fortifications, signaling that Cornwallis wished to surrender.

Cornwallis Surrenders

Cornwallis hoped that Washington would allow him to surrender and return with his troops to Great Britain. But Washington was firm: All of Cornwallis's troops would become prisoners of war. The next day, October 19, Lieutenant General Cornwallis did not appear to make the formal surrender. He sent a junior officer, Brigadier General Charles O'Hara, in his place. O'Hara attempted to offer his surrender to the French commander, who indicated that General Washington was in charge. O'Hara then rode to Washington and surrendered, apologizing, as he did, for the missing Cornwallis.

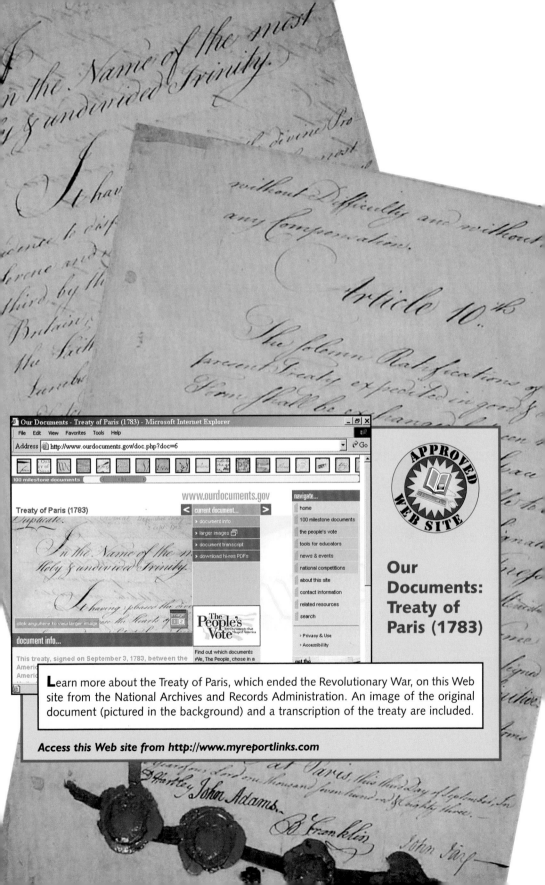

Our Documents: Treaty of Paris (1783)

Learn more about the Treaty of Paris, which ended the Revolutionary War, on this Web site from the National Archives and Records Administration. An image of the original document (pictured in the background) and a transcription of the treaty are included.

Access this Web site from http://www.myreportlinks.com

O'Hara and his defeated army—over 7,200 soldiers and 840 seamen—were then marched to prison camps in Virginia and Maryland. They had fought the last battle of the Revolutionary War on American soil.

The End of the Revolution

Neither the American nor British government believed that the Revolutionary War ended at Yorktown. From the American point of view, the British still held New York, Charleston, and Savannah and were capable of attacking American forces. On the other side, George III and Parliament, England's governing body, were unwilling to accept the idea of defeat.

Other battles between Britain and combined French and Spanish troops took place in the West Indies and in India. In 1782, the British government signaled that it had had enough and wished to end the war. Negotiations took many months and involved two peace treaties. The first was signed on November 30, 1782; it concerned peace between the United States and Great Britain. The final Treaty of Paris, signed on September 3, 1783, involved agreements between Great Britain, France, and Spain.

THE SOLDIERS SPEAK

Many different groups of soldiers fought in the Revolutionary War. Not only were there regular soldiers from the American and British armies, but militiamen from both countries as well. In addition, soldiers came from France and Germany. Finally,

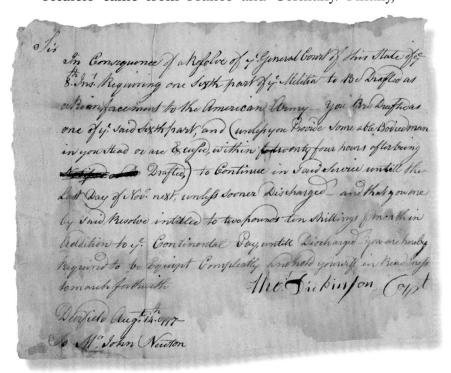

▲ A draft notice sent by the Continental Army to John Newton, a member of the Massachusetts militia. With so many more militiamen than regular soldiers, the Continental Army constantly needed reinforcements—and had to get them through a draft.

American Indians and African Americans became part of the fighting forces on both sides.

Colonial Militia and Continental Army

When the first skirmishes of the Revolutionary War took place, the colonists did not have a regular army. Instead, they relied on militias. Any man between the age of sixteen and fifty could be called to fight, and each colony had its own militia. About one third of the men of any militia were handpicked to be Minutemen. These men were trained to be ready at a moment's notice and would be the first to respond to the alarm.

Although the militias were helpful throughout the war, they were not well trained. They performed well in raids and less conventional battles. They did not do well, however, in the traditional and regimented European-style battles that the English were used to fighting.

A few days before the Battle of Bunker Hill, members of the Second Continental Congress authorized the formation of a short-term army. This seventeen-thousand-man Continental Force under the command of George Washington required only a one-year contract from soldiers, which meant that each year another recruitment drive was necessary. Most of the soldiers in this force came from New England.

It took until September 26, 1776, for the full-fledged Continental Army to be created. Soldiers in

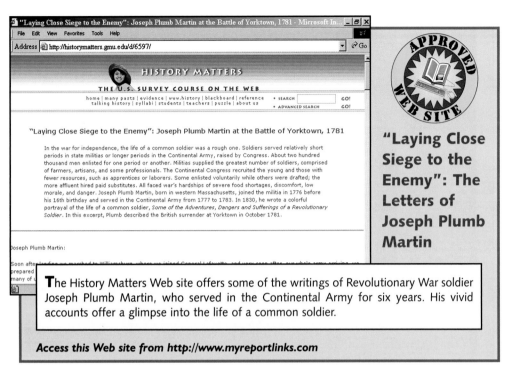

"Laying Close Siege to the Enemy": Joseph Plumb Martin at the Battle of Yorktown, 1781 - Microsoft In...

File   Edit   View   Favorites   Tools   Help

Address http://historymatters.gmu.edu/d/6597/   Go

HISTORY MATTERS

THE U.S. SURVEY COURSE ON THE WEB

home | many pasts | evidence | www.history | blackboard | reference   • SEARCH   GO!
talking history | syllabi | students | teachers | puzzle | about us   • ADVANCED SEARCH   GO!

"Laying Close Siege to the Enemy": Joseph Plumb Martin at the Battle of Yorktown, 1781

In the war for independence, the life of a common soldier was a rough one. Soldiers served relatively short periods in state militias or longer periods in the Continental Army, raised by Congress. About two hundred thousand men enlisted for one period or another. Militias supplied the greatest number of soldiers, comprised of farmers, artisans, and some professionals. The Continental Congress recruited the young and those with fewer resources, such as apprentices or laborers. Some enlisted voluntarily while others were drafted; the more affluent hired paid substitutes. All faced war's hardships of severe food shortages, discomfort, low morale, and danger. Joseph Plumb Martin, born in western Massachusetts, joined the militia in 1776 before his 16th birthday and served in the Continental Army from 1777 to 1783. In 1830, he wrote a colorful portrayal of the life of a common soldier, *Some of the Adventures, Dangers and Sufferings of a Revolutionary Soldier*. In this excerpt, Plumb described the British surrender at Yorktown in October 1781.

Joseph Plumb Martin:

Soon after landing we marched to Williamsburg, where we joined General Lafayette, and very soon after, our whole army arriving, we prepared to...

"Laying Close Siege to the Enemy": The Letters of Joseph Plumb Martin

The History Matters Web site offers some of the writings of Revolutionary War soldier Joseph Plumb Martin, who served in the Continental Army for six years. His vivid accounts offer a glimpse into the life of a common soldier.

Access this Web site from http://www.myreportlinks.com

the Continental Army would be required to serve until the war was over, or no more than three years. This time, soldiers would come from all of the colonies and serve in one of three armies: Northern, Main, and Southern. Although the Continental Congress authorized the army to have seventy-five thousand soldiers, it never grew above eighteen thousand men.

Fifteen-year-old Joseph Plumb Martin enlisted as a Connecticut state trooper serving in the Continental Army in June 1776 against his grandparents' wishes. Sent to New York, he recorded in his diary what his new life as a soldier was like: "I was called out every morning at reveille beating, which was at daybreak, to go to our regimental

parade . . . and there practice the manual exercise."[1]
A short time later, he was ferried to Long Island,
where he encountered American troops returning
from a battle with the British.

We now began to meet the wounded men . . . some
with broken bones, some with broken legs, and some
with broken heads. The sight of these a little daunted
[scared] me, and made me think of home. . . .

We . . . pressed forward towards a creek, where a
large party of Americans and British were engaged [in
battle]. By the time we arrived, the enemy had driven
our men into the creek. . . . Many of them were killed
in the pond, and more were drowned. Some of us went
into the water . . . and took out a number of corpses. . . .[2]

Getting enough soldiers to sign up for the army
was not always easy. Englishman Nicholas Cresswell,
who had come to America in 1774 for an adventure
that lasted until 1777, traveled through Virginia,
New York, and other colonies during the early part of
the war, and he kept a diary of his journey. Obviously
opposed to the Americans, he observed how difficult
it was for the Continental Army's recruiters.

Monday, January 6, 1777. News that Washington had
taken 760 Hessian prisoners at Trenton. . . . Hope it is
a lie. . . .

Tuesday, January 7, 1777. The news is confirmed. The
minds of the people [the colonists] are much altered.
A few days ago they had given up the cause [of inde-
pendence] for lost. Their late successes have turned

the scale and now they are all liberty-mad again. Their recruiting parties could not get a man (except he bought him from his master) no longer since than last week, and now the men are coming in by companies. . . . This has given them new spirits . . . and will prolong the war, perhaps for two years.[3]

Life in the Continental Army was not easy. Because the Continental Congress had little money, many of the soldiers were not paid and received little food. In January 1781, troops from Pennsylvania and New Jersey regiments mutinied when they heard that money was being paid to new recruits.

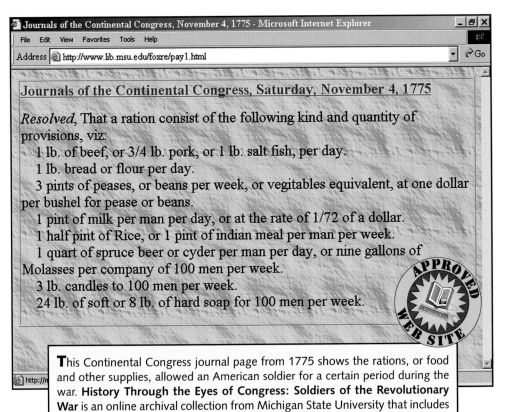

Journals of the Continental Congress, November 4, 1775 - Microsoft Internet Explorer

File   Edit   View   Favorites   Tools   Help

Address 🔊 http://www.lib.msu.edu/foxre/pay1.html   🔗 Go

Journals of the Continental Congress, Saturday, November 4, 1775

Resolved, That a ration consist of the following kind and quantity of provisions, viz:

   1 lb. of beef, or 3/4 lb. pork, or 1 lb. salt fish, per day.
   1 lb. bread or flour per day.
   3 pints of peases, or beans per week, or vegitables equivalent, at one dollar per bushel for pease or beans.
   1 pint of milk per man per day, or at the rate of 1/72 of a dollar.
   1 half pint of Rice, or 1 pint of indian meal per man per week.
   1 quart of spruce beer or cyder per man per day, or nine gallons of Molasses per company of 100 men per week.
   3 lb. candles to 100 men per week.
   24 lb. of soft or 8 lb. of hard soap for 100 men per week.

APPROVED WEB SITE

This Continental Congress journal page from 1775 shows the rations, or food and other supplies, allowed an American soldier for a certain period during the war. **History Through the Eyes of Congress: Soldiers of the Revolutionary War** is an online archival collection from Michigan State University that includes letters, journals, and other primary source documents.

French Troops

On February 6, 1778, France joined in an alliance with the United States. The battles at Saratoga had helped convince them that the Americans could inflict damage on the British. After its defeat by Britain in the French and Indian War, France was eager to help the United States against its enemy. As a result, the French provided the colonies with money, ammunition, and supplies as well as its army and navy. The involvement of the French increased the scope of the war, so that Great Britain not only had to fight in America but throughout the world.

Not all Americans were pleased with this turn of events. In a letter, Major Samuel Shaw discussed his grave concerns about accepting help from France:

> By Heavens! if our rulers had any modesty, they would blush at the idea of calling in foreign aid! 'tis really abominable, that we should send to France for soldiers, when there are so many sons of America idle.[4]

British Army Troops

At the time of the Revolutionary War, Great Britain had a large and well-trained army of approximately forty-eight thousand men worldwide. This highly disciplined force was superior in many ways to American forces, but because they were stationed so far from home, British troops had problems obtaining ammunition, weapons, and food. When supplies did not arrive in time, they resorted to plundering,

 This British cartoon, printed in 1777, depicts British officers at a military academy as childlike competitors for the prize of a command in the war with the American colonies.

or stealing supplies from private citizens, which gave them a bad reputation.

British lieutenant Martin Hunter gave a vivid description of British troops engaged in battle at Cliveden, Pennsylvania, during the battle for Philadelphia, which the British won.

> On our charging they gave way on all sides but again and again they renewed the attack with fresh troops and greater force. We charged them twice, till the battalion was so reduced by killed and wounded, that the bugle was sounded to retreat. . . . This was the first time we had retreated before the Americans, and it was with great difficulty to get our men to obey our orders.[5]

Loyalist Soldiers

The American colonists who remained loyal to Britain after the war began might not have always agreed with British policies of taxation, but they did not believe that the colonies should become independent. Not every Loyalist was a soldier, but many colonists who supported Great Britain were willing to fight the American Patriots. Loyalists had been harassed for some time, enduring threats from mobs and tarring and feathering by those most fervently seeking independence.

Some of the most vicious fighting of the war was between Loyalists and American Patriots. One battle involving Loyalist forces against American militiamen was Kings Mountain, fought in South Carolina on October 7, 1780. Led by a Scottish-born major named Patrick Ferguson, the Loyalist troops had been recruited from the backwoods of the southern colonies, but they were soundly defeated at Kings Mountain.

Sixteen-year-old James Collins, who fought with the American militia that day, recorded what happened to the Loyalists after Major Ferguson was killed:

After the fight was over, . . . the dead lay in heaps on all sides, while the groans of the wounded were heard in every direction. . . . "Great God!" said I, "Is this the fate of mortals, or was it for this cause that man was brought into the world?"

Next morning, which was Sunday, the scene became really distressing; the wives and children of the poor Tories [Loyalists] came in, in great numbers. Their husbands, fathers, and brothers, lay dead in heaps, while others lay wounded or dying; a melancholy sight indeed![6]

American Indians

American Indian tribes fought on both sides of the Revolutionary War, though they were often reluctant to become involved. The Cherokee, the Choctaw, and most of the Iroquois nations (the Mohawk, the Onondoga, the Cayuga, and the Seneca) fought with the British. Only the Oneida and Tuscarora took the side of the American Patriots.

The Americans tried to get Indian tribes to join the fight on their side. Ethan Allen, on his way to the Battle of Quebec, tried to convince the Western Abenaki tribe living by the Canadian border to join with him:

I always love Indians and have hunted a great deal with them I know how to shute and ambush just like Indians and want your Warriors to come and see me and help me fight Regulars [that is, British Army troops]—you know they stand all along close together Rank and file and my men fight so as Indians do and I want your Warriors to join with me and my Warriors like brothers and ambush the Regulars. . . .[7]

American Indians were urged by the colonists to remain neutral if they were not going to join the

Patriots' cause. At first, this tactic was successful. In the end, though, the British were more successful. Though there were many reasons, an American Indian would not have had to look much further than the Declaration of Independence itself, which read in part that the king of England has caused "domestic insurrections amongst us, and has endeavored to bring on the inhabitants of our frontiers, the merciless Indian savages, whose known rule of warfare, is undistinguished destruction of all ages, sexes and conditions." The British recruiting of native people became one more justification for Americans to declare their independence.

The British also provided incentives to native tribes. Not only did British agents offer American

The Captain Johann von Ewald Diaries:
Maps of the Revolutionary War

The Captain Johann von Ewald Diaries:

Maps of the Revolutionary War

Detail of artwork from a map of the Province of New Jersey, 1777.

Captain Johann von Ewald, a Hessian officer, fought with British forces during the Revolutionary War. Twenty-nine maps that he made during the war can be viewed at this university Web site.

Access this Web site from http://www.myreportlinks.com

Indians clothing, cooking utensils, weapons, and ammunition, but they also offered to pay a bonus for each scalp of an American fighter brought to the agent.[8] Raiding parties and massacres took place on all sides. In the end, American Indian nations were caught in the middle of two larger military forces and suffered as a result.

Hessians

As the war began, the British found that they did not have enough troops to fight the American Patriots. As it had done in previous wars, the British government turned to Germany for troops, and most of these men were referred to as Hessians. Almost thirty thousand Hessians fought in the Revolutionary War.

The Hessians were generally mercenaries—hired to fight. They often had no particular political interest in fighting the war. Their interest was in getting paid, and a number of them also deserted. Because they lacked discipline and incentive, they were considered by General Washington to be the weak link in Britain's military, and he specifically targeted them, as at Trenton. Many British soldiers felt the same. After British lieutenant William Hale read a newspaper article about the hiring of Germans, he commented:

I believe . . . their slowness is of the greatest disadvantage in a country almost covered with woods, and against an Enemy whose chief qualification is agility in

▲ Lord Dunmore, Virginia's royal governor, tried to entice African Americans to serve with the British by promising slaves freedom. This print shows Dunmore's flight—he spent much of the war aboard a British ship.

running from fence to fence and thence keeping up an irregular, but galling fire on troops who advance with the same pace as at their exercise. . . . They will not readily fight without being supported by their cannon which we think a useless encumbrance.[9]

The American forces also did not like the Hessians because they often stole supplies, ransacking houses and farms. Although all troops did this, the Hessians developed a reputation for being the worst offenders. John McCasland, who served in the Pennsylvania militia and the Continental Army, recalled an episode when he was chosen to shoot a Hessian looter.

I did not like to shoot a man down in cold blood. The company present knew I was a good marksman, and I concluded to break his thigh. I shot with a rifle and aimed at his hip. He had a large iron tobacco box in his breeches pocket, and I hit the box, the ball glanced, and it entered his thigh and scaled the bone of the thigh on the outside.[10]

African Americans

African Americans served on both sides of the Revolutionary War. No matter which side they chose, they fought for their own freedom as well.

In November 1775, Virginia's royal governor, John Murray, the Earl of Dunmore, offered slaves freedom if they chose to fight for the British:

And I do hereby . . . declare all indented Servants, Negroes, or others, . . . free that are able and willing to bear arms, they joining His Majesty's Troops as soon as may be, for the more speedily reducing this colony to a proper sense of their duty, to His Majesty's crown and dignity.[11]

American leaders were concerned about Lord Dunmore's proclamation and tried to prevent slaves from running away. One newspaper estimated that in less than one month's time, over two thousand slaves had run away to join the British Army. The Virginia Assembly responded in December 1775, with a declaration:

. . . it is enacted, that all negro or other slaves, conspiring to rebel or make insurrection, shall suffer death, and be excluded all benefit of clergy: We think it proper to declare, that all slaves who have been, or shall be seduced, by his lordship's [Lord Dunmore's] proclamation . . . to desert their masters' service, and take up arms against the inhabitants of this colony, shall be liable to such punishment. . . . And to that end all such, who have taken this unlawful and wicked step, may return in safety to their duty, and escape the punishment due to their crimes, we hereby promise pardon to them. . . .[12]

One Virginia plantation owner named Landon Carter kept a diary in which he wrote about how his slaves had run away:

A portrait of an African-American sailor during the Revolutionary War. **Africans in America: The Revolutionary War,** a PBS Web page, provides this image and others as well as primary source accounts of black men who fought for the colonies and those who fought for the Crown.

Last night after going to bed, Moses, my son's man, Joe, Billy, Postillion John, Mulatto Peter; Tom Panticoe, Manuel, and Lancaster Sam ran away, to be sure, to Lord Dunmore, for they got privately into [my son's] room before dark and took out [his] gun and one I had there, too, out of his drawer . . . They took my grandson Landon's bag of bullets and all the Powder, and went off. . . . These accursed villains have stolen Landon's silver buckles, my grandson George's shirts, Tom Parker's new waistcoat and breeches. . . .[13]

Carter longed to hear that his eight fugitive slaves had been captured. He was so distraught that he even described in his diary some of the dreams he had about his slaves.[14] Carter died in December 1778, however, without knowing what had happened to them. Seventeen slaves owned by George Washington left Mount Vernon, his plantation in Virginia, in 1781.

Many African Americans fought on the side of the British. Some joined special army units called the Black Pioneers. But British motives were not always honorable, and many former slaves who fought for the British were never freed. A Hessian army officer named Johann von Ewald commented on this practice in his diary:

> . . . Lord Cornwallis had permitted each [junior officer] to keep two horses and one Negro, each captain, four horses and two Negroes, and so on, according to rank. But since this order was not strictly carried out, the greatest abuse arose from this arrangement. . . . Yes, indeed, I can testify that every soldier had his Negro, who carried his provisions and bundles.[15]

At the final battle of Yorktown, where more than four thousand African Americans supported the British troops, they were given inferior rations. When food ran out, the British forced them out of the battlements into an area between the two sides, where many died.

NEWS OF THE BATTLES

Before the war even began, newspapers in the colonies published articles that cast the British in the worst possible light. These articles documented what was happening at the time, but they also inflamed public opinion.

In the following article, published in the March 30, 1775, edition of the *New York Journal,* the author describes how a colonist who wanted to buy a firelock, a gun, was arrested by British soldiers, tried, and then tarred and feathered, a punishment that was supposed to be forbidden:

Yesterday [March 8], an honest countryman was inquiring for a firelock, when a soldier hearing him, said he had one he would sell. Away goes the ignoramus, and after paying the soldier very honestly for the gun . . . a dozen seized him and hurried the poor fellow away under guard, for a breach of the act against trading with the soldiers. After keeping him in duress [in custody, under force] all night . . . the officers condemned him without a hearing to be tarred and feathered, which sentence has been executed.

After stripping him naked and covering him with tar and feathers, they mounted him on a one-horse truck, and . . . exhibited him as a spectacle through the principal streets of the town. They fixed a label on

In this cartoon from 1774, Bostonians "pay" the excise-man, or tax collector, by pouring tea down his throat after tarring and feathering him. In the background, tea is dumped into the harbor, an obvious reference to the Boston Tea Party.

the man's back, on which was written AMERICAN LIBERTY or A SPECIMEN DEMOCRACY; and to add to the insult they played Yankee Doodle:—Oh Britain, how art thou fallen! . . . What a wretched figure will the Boston expedition hereafter make in the historic page![1]

The First Shots

By the time the war began, the Americans faced an enormous battlefront with a volunteer and poorly trained militia.

An observer of the militiamen described their appearance as they paraded before Colonel William Prescott the evening before the Battle of Bunker Hill, June 16, 1775.

To a man, they wore small clothes, coming down and fastening just below the knee, and long stockings with cowhide shoes ornamented by large buckles, while not a pair of boots graced the company. The coats and waistcoats were loose and of huge dimensions . . . and their shirts were all made of flax, and like every other part of their dress, were homespun. On their heads was worn a large round top and broad brimmed hat. Their arms [weapons] were as various as their costume; here an old soldier carried a heavy Queen's arm, which had done service at the Conquest of Canada twenty years previous, while by his side walked a stripling boy with a Spanish fusee. . . .[2]

At least fourteen African Americans fought on the side of the colonists at Bunker Hill. One, Salem Poor, was responsible for the death of British major

John Pitcairn. Because many colonists did not want black soldiers fighting for the freedom of white colonists, Poor's accomplishment was likely to go unrewarded.[3] Fourteen officers wrote a petition on his behalf.

> We declare that A Negro Man Called Salem Poor of Col. Frye's regiment . . . in the late Battle at Charlestown behaved like an Experienced officer, as Well as an Excellent Soldier. . . . The Reward due to so great and Distinguished a Character, We Submit to the Congress.[4]

The officers' petition fell on deaf ears. By November 12, 1775, General George Washington announced that African-Americans, young boys, and old men would be barred from the military and that no African-American soldiers then in the Army would be allowed to reenlist. Although Washington changed his mind by the end of December 1775 and was willing to allow freed African Americans to enlist, Congress eventually overruled him. As Congress said in January 1776, ". . . free Negroes who have served faithfully in the army [in Boston] may be re-enlisted therein, but no others."[5]

The argument over whether African Americans could serve in the Army continued. Some states ended up permitting such enlistments. Connecticut law allowed a man and his son to avoid the draft if their male slave enlisted in their place. Southern colonies such as South Carolina and Georgia voted against allowing African Americans to join the Army. But South Carolina agreed to let African Americans join the Navy, perhaps because sailors were not allowed to carry weapons.

▲ The uniforms of the Continental Army's infantry, after 1779.

▷ "What Brave Fellows"

When the battleground shifted farther south to New York, approximately twenty thousand British and Hessian troops faced about fourteen thousand American soldiers commanded by General George Washington on August 22, 1776. During the one-day Battle of Long Island, Washington's men attempted to stop the British advance toward New York City. However, the Americans were soundly defeated and ended up retreating to New York City.

Eventually, the British took New York City and moved north. As the Americans retreated toward White Plains in October, the poorly supplied American troops suffered. Soldier Joseph Plumb Martin described how he spent the cold October

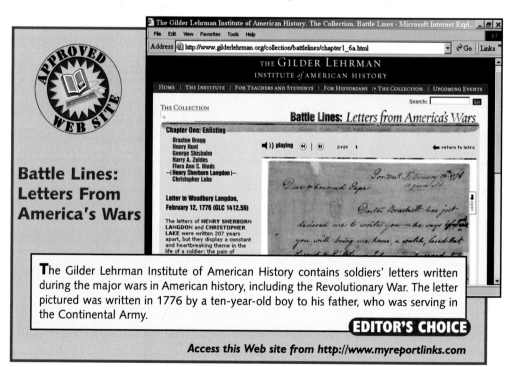

Battle Lines: Letters From America's Wars

The Gilder Lehrman Institute of American History contains soldiers' letters written during the major wars in American history, including the Revolutionary War. The letter pictured was written in 1776 by a ten-year-old boy to his father, who was serving in the Continental Army.

EDITOR'S CHOICE

Access this Web site from http://www.myreportlinks.com

nights before the Battle of White Plains: "I have often, while upon guard, lain on one side until the upper side smarted with cold, then turned that side down to the place warmed by my body, and let the other take its turn at smarting. . . ."[6]

Promoting Courage in New Jersey

Following his surprise attack on the Hessian soldiers stationed at Trenton on Christmas Eve 1776, General Washington and his army used another trick to defeat the British at Princeton on January 3 and 4. An American Army sergeant, known only as Sergeant R___, kept a record of his impressions of these battles in New Jersey. After the Battle of Princeton, he described the prisoners the Americans had captured.

> . . . a haughty, crabbed set of men, as they fully exhibited on their march to the country. In this battle, my pack, which was made fast by leather strings, was shot from my back, and with it went what little clothing I had. It was, however, soon replaced by one which belonged to a British officer, and was well furnished. It was not mine for long, for it was stolen shortly afterwards.[7]

British Difficulties at Saratoga

American brigadier general John Glover fought in both of the battles at Saratoga. A letter that Glover wrote between the battles gives a good impression

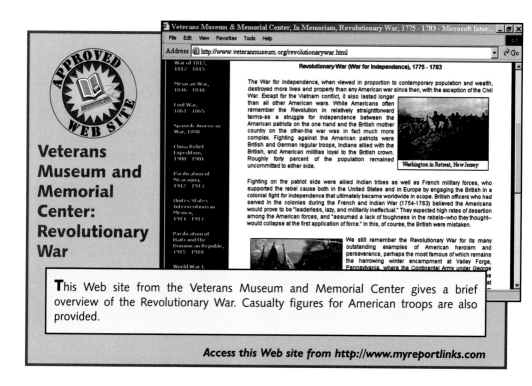

Veterans Museum and Memorial Center: Revolutionary War

Revolutionary War (War for Independence), 1775 - 1783

The War for Independence, when viewed in proportion to contemporary population and wealth, destroyed more lives and property than any American war since then, with the exception of the Civil War. Except for the Vietnam conflict, it also lasted longer than all other American wars. While Americans often remember the Revolution in relatively straightforward terms-as a struggle for independence between the American patriots on the one hand and the British mother country on the other-the war was in fact much more complex. Fighting against the American patriots were British and German regular troops, Indians allied with the British, and American militias loyal to the British crown. Roughly forty percent of the population remained uncommitted to either side.

Washington in Retreat, New Jersey

Fighting on the patriot side were allied Indian tribes as well as French military forces, who supported the rebel cause both in the United States and in Europe by engaging the British in a colonial fight for independence that ultimately became worldwide in scope. British officers who had served in the colonies during the French and Indian War (1754-1763) believed the Americans would prove to be "leaderless, lazy, and militarily ineffectual." They expected high rates of desertion among the American forces, and "assumed a lack of toughness in the rebels--who they thought--would collapse at the first application of force." In this, of course, the British were mistaken.

We still remember the Revolutionary War for its many outstanding examples of American heroism and perseverance, perhaps the most famous of which remains the harrowing winter encampment at Valley Forge, Pennsylvania, where the Continental Army under George

This Web site from the Veterans Museum and Memorial Center gives a brief overview of the Revolutionary War. Casualty figures for American troops are also provided.

Access this Web site from http://www.myreportlinks.com

of the difficulties faced by British general Burgoyne and his troops. Written on September 29, 1777, the letter describes the outcome of the Battle of Bemis Heights, ten days earlier:

We have taken 30 prisoners since the battle, and as many more deserted.

Our men are in fine spirits, are very bold and daring, a proof of which I will give you in an instance two nights past.

I ordered 100 men from my Brigade to take off a picket of about 60 of the enemy, who were posted about half a mile from me, at the same time ordered a covering party of 200 to support them. . . . When I made the proper disposition for the attack, they went on like so many tigers, bidding defiance to musket balls and bayonets. Drove the enemy, killed 3, and wounded a great number more, took one prisoner, 8 Packs, 8 Blankets, 2 guns, 1 sword, and many other articles of Plunder without any loss on our side.

Burgoyne has only 20 days provision. He must give us battle in a day or two, or else retire back.[8]

The Cruel Winter at Valley Forge

During the winter of 1777–1778, the Continental Army faced one of its worst crises. The army was camped in its winter quarters at Valley Forge, Pennsylvania, some twenty miles northwest of Philadelphia, a city still under British control. The soldiers were tired and hungry, and there was no shelter. Their clothing and shoes, if they had any, were tattered. They were ill equipped to survive a harsh Pennsylvania winter. Soldier Joseph Plumb Martin described the march to Valley Forge:

The army was now not only starved but naked; the greatest part were not only shirtless and barefoot, but destitute of all other clothing, especially blankets. I procured a small piece of raw cowhide and made myself a pair of moccasins, which kept my feet (while they lasted) from the frozen ground. . . .[9]

Albigence Waldo, a surgeon with the Continental Army, kept a journal of that winter that describes the misery of the Americans at Valley Forge.

▲ *General George Washington and the Marquis de Lafayette at their winter quarters in Valley Forge, Pennsylvania.*

December 14.—. . . I am Sick—discontented—and out of humor. Poor food—hard lodging—Cold Weather—fatigue—Nasty Cloaths—nasty Cookery—Vomit half my time—. . . I can't Endure it—Why are we sent here to starve and Freeze—I am Sick, my feet lame, my legs are sore, my body cover'd with this tormenting Itch—my Cloaths are worn out, my Constitution is broken, my former Activity is exhausted by fatigue, hunger & Cold, I fail fast I shall soon be no more![10]

▷ Fighting at Kings Mountain

As the fighting shifted to the southern colonies, a number of unforgettable battles took place. One of the most famous was at Kings Mountain, in South Carolina, which pitted two armies of militiamen, one Patriot and one Loyalist, in a heated battle.

Thomas Young, a sixteen-year-old private fighting for the Patriots, described in his memoir what happened:

On top of the mountain, in the thickest of the fight, I saw Colonel Williams fall, and a braver or better man never died upon the field of battle. . . . They carried him into a tent, and sprinkled some water in his face. He revived, and his first words were, "For God's sake, boys, don't give up the hill!" . . . I left him in the arms of his son, Daniel, and returned to the field to revenge his fate.[11]

Yorktown: A Critical and Precarious Situation

During the siege at Yorktown, Virginia, the American forces were able to set up their artillery batteries to devastating effect. They occupied outlying redoubts left by the British and dug trenches that inched closer to the British positions. American surgeon James Thatcher recorded his thoughts about the action:

The siege is daily becoming more and more formidable and alarming, and his Lordship [Cornwallis, the British commander] must view his situation as extremely critical, if not desperate. Being in the trenches every other night and day, I have a fine opportunity of witnessing the sublime and stupendous scene which is continually exhibiting. The bombshells from the besiegers and the besieged are incessantly crossing each other's path in the air. They are clearly visible in the form of a black ball in the day, but in the night they appear like a fiery meteor with a blazing tail, most beautifully brilliant, ascending majestically from the mortar to a certain altitude, and gradually descending to the spot where they are destined to execute their work of destruction. . . .[12]

The British artillery inflicted a great deal of damage as well. Joseph Plumb Martin remembered what happened to a sergeant from New York as the American trenches were shelled by the British.

I was sitting on the side of the trench, when some of the New York troops coming in, one of the sergeants

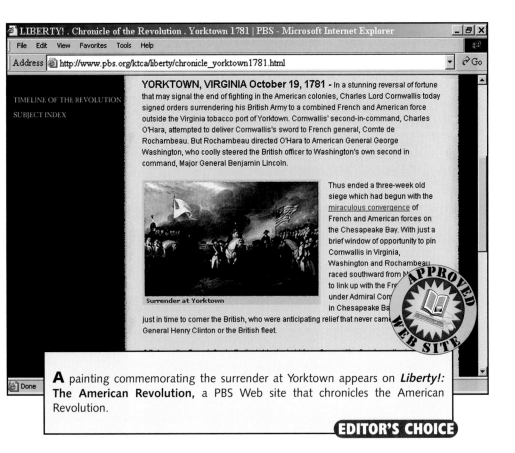

YORKTOWN, VIRGINIA October 19, 1781 - In a stunning reversal of fortune that may signal the end of fighting in the American colonies, Charles Lord Cornwallis today signed orders surrendering his British Army to a combined French and American force outside the Virginia tobacco port of Yorktown. Cornwallis' second-in-command, Charles O'Hara, attempted to deliver Cornwallis's sword to French general, Comte de Rochambeau. But Rochambeau directed O'Hara to American General George Washington, who coolly steered the British officer to Washington's own second in command, Major General Benjamin Lincoln.

Thus ended a three-week old siege which had begun with the miraculous convergence of French and American forces on the Chesapeake Bay. With just a brief window of opportunity to pin Cornwallis in Virginia, Washington and Rochambeau raced southward from N to link up with the Fre under Admiral Cor in Chesapeake Ba just in time to corner the British, who were anticipating relief that never came General Henry Clinton or the British fleet.

Surrender at Yorktown

A painting commemorating the surrender at Yorktown appears on *Liberty!: The American Revolution,* a PBS Web site that chronicles the American Revolution.

EDITOR'S CHOICE

stepped up to the breastwork to look about him; the enemy threw a small shell which fell upon the outside of the works; the man turned his face to look at it; at that instant a shot from the enemy . . . passed just by his face without touching him at all; he fell dead into the trench; I put my hand on his forehead and found his skull was shattered all in pieces, . . . but not a particle of skin was broken.[13]

The shelling and the lack of supplies proved to be too much for the British. Without getting help from the Royal Navy, Cornwallis was trapped at Yorktown. On October 15, 1781, after British troops had lost two more of their redoubts, which placed American troops within three hundred yards of the British forces, General Cornwallis wrote, "The safety of the place is . . . so precarious that I cannot recommend that the fleet [Royal Navy] and army should run the great risque in endeavoring to save us."[14] After a few more days of heavy shelling, Cornwallis surrendered.

THE WOMEN OF THE REVOLUTIONARY WAR

Historians are continually finding previously undiscovered documents or ones that were overlooked in their search for a more complete story of what happened during the Revolutionary War.

That is why we now know more about the role that women played during the war. The few women

▲ The story of Molly Pitcher's courage and bravery on the battlefield is well known. The stories of other American women who suffered through the Revolutionary War, though less famous, can be found in their letters, diaries, and journals.

usually mentioned in histories about the war are Abigail Adams, Betsy Ross, and Molly Pitcher.[1] In the last thirty years, historians have found primary source documents such as letters, diaries, and journals that shed light on what life was like for other women during America's war for independence.

Anne Hulton

Anne Hulton, a British Loyalist living in Boston, was the sister of a commissioner of customs in that city. Although she did not live in Boston long, she wrote letters to friends and family back home. Most were written to Mrs. Adam Lightbody, a friend living in Liverpool, England. Hulton returned to England in 1775. Her letters provide one Loyalist's view of the events leading up to the Revolutionary War. In this letter to Mrs. Lightbody, Anne Hulton describes the skirmishes at Lexington and Concord:

The Troops went on to Concord & executed the business they were sent on, & on their return found two or three of their people Lying in the Agonies of Death, scalp'd & their Noses & ears cut off & Eyes bored out—Which exasperated the Soldiers exceedingly—

. . . Stone Walls Served as a cover to the Rebels, from whence they fired on the Troops. . . . In this manner were the Troops harassed in their return for Seven or eight Miles . . . when to their great joy they were relieved by a Brigade . . . under the command of Lord Percy with two pieces of Artillery. The Troops now combated with fresh Ardour, . . . receiving Sheets of fire . . . for many Miles, yet having no visible Enemy . . . for they never would face 'em in an open field, but

always skulked & fired from behind Walls, & trees, & out of Windows of Houses, but this cost them dear for the Soldiers entered those dwellings, & put all the Men to death. . . .[2]

Grace Growden Galloway

The circumstances of war made life difficult enough for happily married people, but when politics separated them, the woman was often the one to suffer. Grace Growden Galloway was from a wealthy Philadelphia family that supported the Patriots'

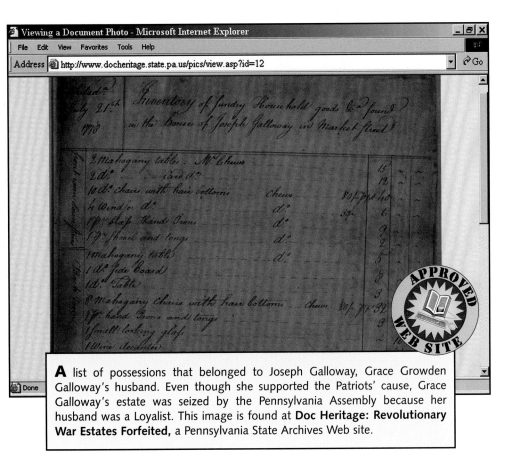

A list of possessions that belonged to Joseph Galloway, Grace Growden Galloway's husband. Even though she supported the Patriots' cause, Grace Galloway's estate was seized by the Pennsylvania Assembly because her husband was a Loyalist. This image is found at **Doc Heritage: Revolutionary War Estates Forfeited,** a Pennsylvania State Archives Web site.

cause. Her husband, Joseph, although a member of the Continental Congress, did not. When that body voted to adopt the Declaration of Independence, Joseph Galloway left for New York. There he joined the British Army and advised General William Howe, wrongly, that most Americans were Loyalists and would support the British Army's suppression of

▲ A woman entertains British soldiers on the porch of her estate during the Revolutionary War. Life for most women in the American colonies, especially those whose husbands were away at war, was much more difficult than this print portrays.

the Colonial rebellion. When the British occupied Philadelphia, Joseph Galloway returned and provided support to British forces. When British troops evacuated the city and marched to New York, he followed, taking their daughter as well. Eventually, the two settled in England.

A Wife Loses Everything

Grace Galloway chose to stay behind, and in doing so, lost everything when Pennsylvania government officials tried to seize her house and her possessions after the British evacuation. In their eyes, she was the wife of a Loyalist, no matter which side she was on. At the time, women had few rights under the law. Unfortunately, she eventually lost her house and even the right to her inheritance from her father, until her husband died. Since she died before him, she never received her inheritance. But she was able to make sure that her daughter finally received it.

In addition to the diaries that Grace Galloway kept, she also wrote poetry. The following poem offers advice to women about marriage. The Revolutionary War had obviously prompted Grace Galloway to have second thoughts about her own position in life and the institution of marriage itself.

> never get Tyed to a Man
> for when once you are yoked
> Tis all a Mere Joke
> of seeing your freedom again.[3]

▷ Sarah Hodgkins

Sarah Hodgkins was left behind with three children when her husband left home. He served almost three full terms in the service of the colonies, one in the Massachusetts militia and two years in the Continental Army. During their separation, they wrote many letters to each other.

On October 19, 1776, in a letter to her husband, Sara Hodgkins confided that she did not want him to reenlist, although she apologized for being so "free" in her displeasure.

I want very much to see you I hope if we Live to see this Campaign out we shall have the happiness of live-ing together again. I dont know what you think about Staying again but I think it cant be inconsistent with your duty to come home to your family it will trouble me very much if you Should ingage again . . . So I hope [you] will excuse my freedom.[4]

Her husband not only enlisted again, he did so for a three-year term. During those years, he visited at times and fathered a fourth child, a son who died while he was away. Her unhappiness was evident in this letter.

I have Looked for you till I know not how to look any longer but I dont know how to give over your not writ-ing to me gives me Some uneasiness for I am sure it is not for want of oppertunities to Send for I have heard of a number of oficers coming home latly. I wrote to

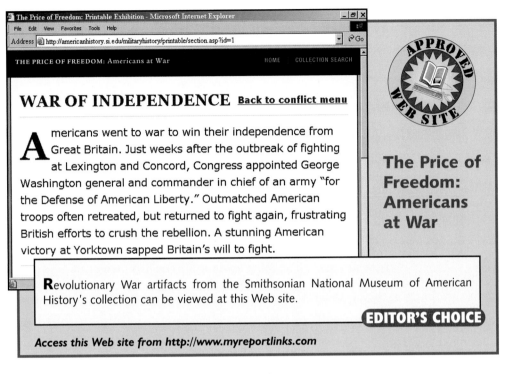

The Price of Freedom: Printable Exhibition - Microsoft Internet Explorer

File Edit View Favorites Tools Help

Address | http://americanhistory.si.edu/militaryhistory/printable/section.asp?id=1 | Go

THE PRICE OF FREEDOM: Americans at War   HOME   COLLECTION SEARCH

WAR OF INDEPENDENCE Back to conflict menu

Americans went to war to win their independence from Great Britain. Just weeks after the outbreak of fighting at Lexington and Concord, Congress appointed George Washington general and commander in chief of an army "for the Defense of American Liberty." Outmatched American troops often retreated, but returned to fight again, frustrating British efforts to crush the rebellion. A stunning American victory at Yorktown sapped Britain's will to fight.

The Price of Freedom: Americans at War

Revolutionary War artifacts from the Smithsonian National Museum of American History's collection can be viewed at this Web site.

EDITOR'S CHOICE

Access this Web site from http://www.myreportlinks.com

you by a post about two months ago & have had no returns Sence I should be glad to know the reason of your not writing to me the first oppertunity you have if it is not too much trouble for you.[5]

Despite the difficulties that her husband's long absences brought about, Sarah Hodgkins worked to provide him with what he needed while he was in the army. Had their letters not survived the war, neither of them would have been known to history.

Eliza Wilkinson

Another woman whose letters have provided a window on what life was like during the war is Eliza Wilkinson, the daughter of a wealthy farmer who lived on the sea islands southeast of Charleston, South Carolina. She endured British soldiers entering her home and stealing her family's clothes.

I ventured to speak to the inhuman monster who had my clothes. I . . . begged him to spare me only a suit or two: but I got nothing but a hearty curse for my pains; nay, so far was his callous heart from relenting, that casting his eyes towards my shoes, 'I want them buckles,' said he; and immediately knelt at my feet to take them out. . . . The other wretches . . . took my sister's earrings from her ears. . . . They took care to tell us, when they were going away, that they had favored us a great deal that we might thank our stars it was no worse.[6]

A brave woman who stood her ground in the face of troops plundering her home, Eliza Wilkinson was just as frustrated with her place in life, as seen in this letter in which she discusses the role of women:

The men say we have no business with them [politics], it is not in our sphere! I won't have it thought that because we are the weaker sex as to bodily strength, my dear, we are capable of nothing more than minding the dairy, visiting the poultry house and all such domestic concerns. . . . They won't even allow us the liberty of thought, and that is all I want. . . .[7]

THE WAR IN SONG AND POETRY

The most famous song at the time of the Revolutionary War was "Yankee Doodle." Surprisingly, both sides used it to boost the morale of their soldiers. The British played the tune during the French and Indian War to make fun of unsophisticated New Englanders, "Yankees," whom they considered country bumpkins, or "doodles." British troops reportedly played the tune as they marched to Lexington and Concord, to mock the colonists. A British verse about a bumpkin who wanted to buy a gun went like this:

> *Yankee Doodle's come to town*
> *For to buy a firelock,*
> *We will tar and feather him*
> *And so will we John Hancock.*[1]

American soldiers made the song their own. Historians know that American soldiers sang this verse at Bunker Hill.

> *Father and I went down to camp,*
> *along with Captain Good'in,*
> *And there we see the men and boys*
> *as thick as hasty puddin'.*

Once Washington received his commission to lead the Continental Army, these verses written about him became popular.

And there was Captain Washington,
And gentlefolks about him,
They say he's grown so tarnal proud,
He will not ride without them.

and

And there was Captain Washington
upon a slapping stallion,
A giving orders to his men;
I guess there was a million.

Many versions of the song have been published, but the chorus is often the same.

Yankee Doodle, keep it up,
Yankee Doodle Dandy,
Mind the Music and the step,
And with the girls be handy.[2]

A Loyalist Song

One song from the Loyalist point of view was "The Rebels." Like "Yankee Doodle," it made fun of the Patriots' hunting shirts and rifles. However, the tone of the song was much more serious than mocking. Its first verse follows.

Ye brave honest subjects who dare to be loyal,
And have stood the brunt of every trial,
Of hunting shirts and rifle guns;

Folk Music of England, Scotland, Ireland, Wales & America: War Songs - Microsoft Internet Explorer

File   Edit   View   Favorites   Tools   Help

Address http://www.contemplator.com/war.html   Go

Folk Music

Of England, Scotland, Ireland, Wales & America

Songs of War

Folk Music of England, Scotland, Ireland, Wales, and America

This Web site offers audio files and lyrics for American and British songs that were popular at the time of the Revolutionary War.

Access this Web site from http://www.myreportlinks.com

Come listen awhile and I'll tell you a song;
I'll show you those Yankees are all in the wrong,
Who, with blustering look and most awkward gait,
'Gainst their lawful sovereign dare for to prate,
With their hunting shirts and rifle guns.[3]

▷ America's Noble Sons

A popular Patriot song, "The Dying Redcoat" attempted to show a British soldier having a change of heart. Set to an old folk tune, the song relates the sad story of a British soldier who comes to America to fight the colonists, only to be mortally wounded. No one knows when the words were written or even who wrote them, but it is said to have been written by a British sergeant when he was wounded in New York on September 16, 1776. As he dies, he praises America's brave soldiers and urges them to fight on—words that any American Patriot longed to hear. The second, third, and last verses follow.

And when to Boston we did come,
We thought by the aid of our British guns,
To drive the rebels from that place,
To fill their hearts with sore disgrace.
But to our sorrow and surprise,
We saw men like grasshoppers rise;
They fought like heroes much enraged,
Which did affright old General Gage.

Like lions roaring of their prey,
They feared no danger or dismay;
Bold British blood runs through their veins,
And still with courage they sustain.
We saw those bold Columbia's sons
Spread death and slaughter from their guns:
Freedom or death! these heroes cry,
They did not seem afraid to die.

Now I've received my mortal wound,
I bid farewell to Old England's ground;
My wife and children will mourn for me,
Whilst I lie cold in America.
Fight on America's noble sons,
Fear not Britannia's thundering guns;
Maintain your cause from year to year,
God's on your side, you need not fear.[4]

Lines written by a Revolutionary Soldier.

On taking a retrospective view of my sufferings while in the Revolutiona·y army, in which I served three years and a half, in which time I suffered with hunger, cold, and want of clothing.

ON the cold earth I oft have lain,
Oppress'd with hunger toil and pain,
While storms and tempests roar'd around,
And frost and snow had cloth'd the ground
  The British troops, did us assail,
  In storms of snow, and rattling hail,
All this with patience long we bore,
Until that sanguine war was o'er,
And Independence made secure,
For which we did those toils endure,
Our hostile foes then left our shore,
Retired for to return no more,—
  Fair freedom now her laurels spread
  O'er hostile fields where warriors bled ;
  No more we hear the din of war,
  Nor thund'ring cannon from a far,
Here peace spreads o'er our fertile plains,
No tyrants shake their galling chains,
Our ships safe o'er the ocean glide,
And waft in wealth with ev'ry tide,
  My friends remember us who bled,
  When on the sanguine fields you tread,
  Nor spurn us if of you we crave,
  Some aid while tot'ring o'er the grave.
Our fleeting days will shortly end,
Then with our native dust we blend,

Death soon will close our languid eyes,
And all our cares beneath the skies :
  Columbia's ~ons who us survive,
  And in this land of freedom live,
  Revere that Providential hand,
  That long has blest your happy land—
Your Constitution ever prize,
Your tow'ring fame will reach the skies,
And while you all in Union blend,
It will from war your shores defend—
  Daily improvements here are made
  For agriculture and for trade,
  Here tow'ring manufactures rise
  Where'er you turn your wand'ring eyes ;
Your treasuries now with gold o'erflow,
Riches abound where'er you go,
No hostile banners you alarm,
You sit at home free from all harm —
  Long may your happy land be blest,
  And you enjoy both peace and rest ;
  Generations yet to come,
  Shall find a lasting peaceful home.
Look back and see what we have done,
Extol the victories we have won,
And when we all in dust shall sleep,
To our memories will long vigils keep,
  And o'er our heads will trophies raise,
  With lasting songs of joy and praise.
  And now my friends a long adieu,
  Our fleeting days are short and few,
  We soon must leave this trying shore.
  And land where time shall be no more.

These verses were written by a Revolutionary War soldier after three and a half years of "hunger, cold, and want of clothing."

Poking Fun at Britain

As with many songs from the Revolutionary War, the person who wrote "The Rich Lady Over the Sea" remains a mystery. The song makes fun of a rich lady over the sea (Great Britain), who wants her daughter (the colonies) to pay a tax on tea. The first, second, third, and last verses follow.

There was a rich lady lived over the sea,
And she was an island queen,
Her daughter lived off in the new country,
With an ocean of water between.
With an ocean of water between.
With an ocean of water between.

The old lady's pockets were filled with gold,
Yet never contented was she,
So she ordered her daughter to pay her a tax,
Of thruppence a pound on the tea.
Of thruppence a pound on the tea.
Of thruppence a pound on the tea.

Oh mother, dear mother, the daughter replied,
I'll not do the thing that you ask,
I'm willing to pay fair price on the tea,
But never the thruppenney tax.
But never the thruppenney tax.
But never the thruppenney tax.

And then she called out to the island queen,
Oh mother, dear mother, called she,
Your tea you may have when 'tis steeped enough,
But never a tax from me!
But never a tax from me!
But never a tax from me![5]

An African-American Poet

Perhaps the most important poet to come out of the Revolutionary War was Phillis Wheatley, a former slave. Taken from the African country of Senegal when she was seven or eight years of age and sold to a tailor in Boston named John Wheatley, Phillis Wheatley became a member of the household and was raised with the Wheatley's two children. Unlike many slaves, she was encouraged to read and write and study Greek, Latin, and the Bible. She was still a teenager when her first poem was published in Boston.

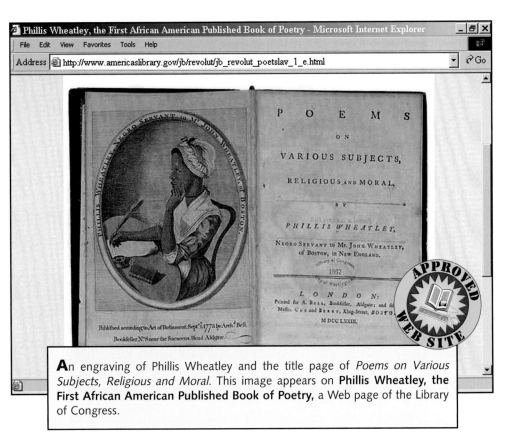

An engraving of Phillis Wheatley and the title page of *Poems on Various Subjects, Religious and Moral*. This image appears on **Phillis Wheatley, the First African American Published Book of Poetry,** a Web page of the Library of Congress.

Wheatley even corresponded with George Washington. The following letter that she sent him included a poem she had written in his honor, to commemorate his being named commander of the Continental Army.

Sir,

I have taken the freedom to address your Excellency in the enclosed poem, and entreat your acceptance, though I am not insensible of its inaccuracies. Your being appointed by the Grand Continental Congress to be Generalissimo of the armies of North America, together with the fame of your virtues, excite sensations not easy to suppress. Your generosity, therefore,

I presume, will pardon the attempt. Wishing your Excellency all possible success in the great cause you are so generously engaged in. I am,

Your Excellency's most obedient humble servant,

Phillis Wheatley.[6]

Here is the last verse of that poem, composed in 1776.

Proceed, great chief, with virtue on thy side,
Thy ev'ry action let the goddess guide.
A crown, a mansion, and a throne that shine,
With gold unfading, WASHINGTON! be thine.[7]

"THE WORLD TURNED UPSIDE DOWN"

Legend has it that a British band played the tune "The World Turned Upside Down" as British forces surrendered to General George Washington at Yorktown, Virginia. The tune's title summed up the feelings of the British military, forced to admit defeat to a small group of Britain's own colonies.

▲ John Adams, Benjamin Franklin, John Jay, and Henry Laurens are pictured, from left to right, in this painting commemorating the signing of the peace treaty with Great Britain that ended the Revolutionary War. British commissioners David Hartley and Richard Oswald are pictured seated at right.

Although many people realized that this victory was important, very few recognized that this battle marked the end of the war.

The British continued to hold Charleston, South Carolina, and New York City. Officials from Great Britain and the United States met in Paris to hammer out a settlement, but the treaty was not agreed on for another year. In November 1782, Great Britain agreed to give the American colonies their independence and to withdraw its remaining troops, but the treaty would not take effect until all countries involved in the conflict had made peace with each other. A few months later, France and Britain agreed on a peaceful end to their differences, as did Spain and Britain. The final treaty was signed on September 3, 1783.

Many in Great Britain lamented the loss of the colonies, perhaps none more so than King George III. He wrote a letter during the 1780s that revealed his thoughts:

America is lost! Must we fall beneath the blow? Or have we resources that may repair the mischief? What are those resources? Should they be sought in distant Regions held by precarious Tenure, or shall we seek them at home in the exertions of a new policy?[1]

George III was so unpopular in Britain by the end of the war that he wrote another letter in which he abdicated, or resigned, his throne. But he never gave his letter to Parliament and ruled as king until his death in 1820.

▶ An Uneasy Peace

Now that the fighting had stopped and victory was achieved, the real work of the country began. But peace did not come easily to the American colonies, especially where Loyalists were concerned. Many Loyalists left the country rather quickly. The rich or well connected went to Great Britain. Others, who had little money, moved to Canada or the Bahamas. Some did return quietly to their communities and tried to resume their lives.

Loyalists who remained behind in the United States sent reports to Great Britain about the state of

The National Archives' Charters of Freedom Web site contains extensive information on the Declaration of Independence, the U.S. Constitution, and the history leading up to the creation of these documents.

EDITOR'S CHOICE

Access this Web site from http://www.myreportlinks.com

affairs when the war was over. One anonymous Loyalist who awaited the British evacuation from New York City wrote:

> . . . the Mob now reigns as fully and uncontrolled as in the Beginning of our Troubles and America is as hostile to Great Britain at this Hour as she was at any Period during the War. . . . The Load of Taxes is intolerable. Farms in general pay a Tax which is greater than the Rents they paid formerly. . . . I am told that upwards of One hundred thousand people . . . have already applied to be transported to Nova Scotia and Canada.[2]

A British officer named Stephen Jarvis returned to his Connecticut home after the war, intending to marry his fiancée. He had been gone for seven years, and even though the war was over, his life was still in danger. Shortly after he returned, a mob arrived at his house. He recorded the scene:

> [I]n a few moments the house was filled [with the mob] . . . I saw many whom I knew, . . . and offered them my hand. Some shook hands with me. Others again damned me for [being] a damned Tory. . . . At last one of them who seemed to be their leader addressed me in these words: "Jarvis, you must leave this town immediately. We won't hurt you now, but if you are seen within thirty miles of this by sundown you must abide the consequences."[3]

Jarvis did not want to leave until he had married his fiancée, so he quickly arranged for a wedding to take place that night. He even invited some of those who had tried to get rid of him. The next morning, Jarvis and his new wife fled before he could be arrested.

▲ *George Washington, who had led thirteen struggling colonies in a fight against one of the world's great powers, went on to lead the new nation as its first president.*

Stepping Down

On December 23, 1783, George Washington appeared before Congress, which was meeting in Annapolis, Maryland, and resigned his commission as general of the Continental Army. He said, in part:

> Having now finished the work assigned me, I retire from the great theatre of Action; and bidding an Affectionate farewell to this August body under whose orders I have so long acted, I here offer my Commission, and take my leave of all the employments of public life.[4]

One man who heard Washington's speech that day, Dr. James McHenry, had worked for Washington during the war. That evening, McHenry wrote a letter to his fiancée, Margaret Caldwell, in which he shared his observations about Washington's speech.

> It was a solemn and affecting spectacle. . . . The spectators all wept, and there was hardly a member of Congress who did not drop tears. The General's hand which held the address shook as he read it. When he spoke of the officers who had composed his family . . . he was obliged to support the paper with both hands. But when he commended the interests of his dearest country to almighty God . . . his voice faultered and sunk, and the whole house felt his agitations.[5]

McHenry closed his letter with the following thoughts:

On December 23, 1783, in the Maryland State House, where Congress then met, General George Washington resigned his commission as Commander in Chief of the Continental Army. His resignation was significant because it ensured a peaceful transfer of power, with civilian rule instead of a military dictatorship.

This is only a sketch of the scene. . . . So many circumstances crowded into view and gave rise to so many affecting emotions. The events of the revolution just accomplished—the new situation into which it had thrown the affairs of the world—the great man who had borne so conspicuous a figure in it . . .—the past— the present—the future—the manner—the occasion— all conspired to render it a spectacle inexpressibly solemn and affecting.[6]

George Washington, the man who had led America's war for independence, would go on to be elected the new nation's first president. With that event, the peaceful transition from commander of the Continental Army to Commander in Chief of the United States, the young democracy was on its way.

Report Links

The Internet sites described below can be accessed at http://www.myreportlinks.com

▶**The Learning Page: The American Revolution, 1763–1783**
Editor's Choice This Library of Congress site contains primary sources of the Revolutionary War.

▶**The Price of Freedom: Americans at War**
Editor's Choice View Revolutionary War artifacts from the National Museum of American History.

▶*Liberty!:* **The American Revolution**
Editor's Choice Learn about the American Revolution from this PBS Web site.

▶**The Charters of Freedom**
Editor's Choice Learn more about the Revolutionary War and the creation of a new nation.

▶**Battle Lines: Letters From America's Wars**
Editor's Choice This Web site contains letters of American soldiers from the Revolutionary War.

▶**"The Decisive Day Is Come:" The Battle of Bunker Hill**
Editor's Choice Read about the Battle of Bunker Hill on this site.

▶**Africans in America: The Revolutionary War**
Learn about the lives and loyalties of African Americans during the Revolutionary War.

▶**The American Revolution**
Maps showing Revolutionary War campaigns can be found on this West Point Web site.

▶**The American Revolution and Its Era: Maps and Charts**
Browse through maps and charts from the Revolutionary War period.

▶**America's Homepage: Paul Revere's Account of His Midnight Ride to Lexington**
Read Paul Revere's account of his midnight ride.

▶**Benjamin Franklin: In His Own Words**
Learn about the life of Benjamin Franklin through primary source documents.

▶**Boston Massacre**
Learn about the Boston Massacre on this Web site.

▶**The Captain Johann von Ewald Diaries: Maps of the Revolutionary War**
View maps made by a Hessian officer during the Revolutionary War.

▶**Digitized Primary American History Sources**
View a collection of primary sources of American history.

▶**Doc Heritage: Revolutionary War Estates Forfeited**
See the documents of a Pennsylvania couple divided by the war.

Report Links

The Internet sites described below can be accessed at http://www.myreportlinks.com

▶**Folk Music of England, Scotland, Ireland, Wales, and America**
Listen to popular songs of the Revolutionary War era.

▶**Hargrett Rare Book & Manuscript Library: Rare Map Collection**
View maps made during America's war for independence.

▶**History Through the Eyes of Congress: Soldiers of the Revolutionary War**
This university Web site offers a glimpse into the lives of Revolutionary War soldiers.

▶**"Laying Close Siege to the Enemy": The Letters of Joseph Plumb Martin**
Read the words of a Revolutionary War soldier.

▶**Legacies: Collecting America's History at the Smithsonian**
Take a tour of Revolutionary War artifacts on this Smithsonian Web site.

▶**The Library of Congress: Today in History: April 19**
Learn about the start of the American Revolution on this Web site.

▶**Named Campaigns—Revolutionary War**
The Army's Center of Military History site gives a brief overview of the battles of the war.

▶**National Park Service Museum Collections: American Revolutionary War**
Explore the history of the American Revolution through National Park Service sites.

▶**Our Documents: Treaty of Paris (1783)**
View the peace treaty that brought the Revolutionary War to an end.

▶**The Papers of George Washington**
Browse the University of Virginia's collection of George Washington's papers.

▶**Phillis Wheatley, the First African American Published Book of Poetry**
Learn about Phillis Wheatley's life and poetry on this Web site.

▶**Pictures of the Revolutionary War**
Find pictures from the Revolutionary War on this National Archives Web site.

▶**Revolutionary America! 1763–1789**
View this virtual exhibit of the Revolutionary War.

▶**Spy Letters of the American Revolution**
Read about espionage during the Revolutionary War.

▶**Veterans Museum and Memorial Center: Revolutionary War**
Read a brief overview of the war on this Web site.

barbarian—An uncivilized person.

cooper—A person who makes or repairs wooden tubs and casks (barrels).

countersign—A secret sign or signal.

crabbed—Ill-tempered.

cutlass—A short, curved sword.

dispatch—Put to death.

duress—Confinement.

encumbrance—Burden.

entrenching—Digging trenches.

expended—Used up.

exulting—Rejoicing.

falter—To hesitate.

firelock—A type of gun.

gall—To chafe or rub against the skin.

grape—Short for "grapeshot," a cluster of small cannonballs.

grenadier—British infantry soldiers.

insurrection—An armed revolt.

militia—Citizens who become involved in military action but are not part of a regular standing army. In the colonies, each colony had its own militia.

minutemen—Militiamen who were trained to take part in military action at a moment's notice.

mutineer—Someone who takes part in a mutiny or revolt.

platoon—A unit of the military.

plunder—To rob during a war.

prate—Chatter.

procure—To obtain or acquire.

Providence—Divine guidance.

Queen's arm—A type of gun.

reconnoiter—To make a preliminary inspection.

redoubts—Temporary fortifications often built of earth.

Regulars—Trained, professional, regular soldiers in an army.

reveille—The first military formation of the day.

sallied—Rushed out.

sentinel—A soldier standing guard; sentry.

skulk—To lurk or hide.

stripling—thin.

thruppence—Three British pence, or pennies.

Tory—An American loyal to Great Britain; a Loyalist.

valor—Bravery.

waistcoat—A short vest.

yoked—Joined together like oxen.

Chapter 1. "The Shot Heard Round the World"

1. Teaching American History Document Library, Paul Revere, "Memorandum on Events of April 18, 1775," n.d., <http://www.teachingamericanhistory.org/library/index.asp?document=874> (February 10, 2006).

2. Ibid.

3. Ibid.

4. Ray Raphael, *A People's History of the American Revolution: How Common People Shaped the Fight for Independence* (New York: The New Press, 2001), p. 49.

5. Hugh F. Rankin, *The American Revolution* (New York: G.P. Putnam's Sons, 1964), pp. 25–26.

6. Paul Revere, *The American Revolution: Writings From the War of Independence* (New York: The Library of America, 2001), p. 4.

7. Deposition of Sylvanus Wood, June 17, 1826, Henry B. Dawson, *Battles of the United States by Sea and Land,* vol. 1 (New York: 1858), pp. 22–23.

8. Ibid.

9. Daniel Marston, *The American Revolution 1774–1783* (Oxford: Osprey Publishing, 2002), p. 28.

10. John C. Dann, ed., *The Revolution Remembered: Eyewitness Accounts of the War for Independence* (Chicago: The University of Chicago Press, 1980), pp. 7–8.

11. Amos Barrett, *The Concord Fight; An Account by Amos Barrett; The Personal Experiences of the Author, Who Participated in the Fight* (Boston: Thomas Todd, 1924), pp. 12–14.

12. Ibid.

13. Rankin, p. 29

14. Ibid., pp. 29–30.

15. Frederick MacKenzie, "Diary, April 18–21, 1775," in *The American Revolution: Writings From the War of Independence,* p. 9.

16. Peter Oliver, "The Origin & Progress of the American Rebellion," in *The American Revolution: Writings From the War of Independence,* p. 26.

17. Ibid., p. 27.

18. MacKenzie, *The American Revolution: Writings From the War of Independence,* p. 11.

19. George Washington, "To Burwell Bassett," in *George Washington: Writings* (New York: Library of America, 1997), p. 169.

Chapter 2. A Brief History of the Revolution

1. Archiving Early America, "The Boston Massacre: A Behind-the-Scenes Look at Paul Revere's Most Famous Engraving," n.d., <http://earlyamerica.com/review/winter96/massacre.html> (September 30, 2005).

2. Robert Middlekauff, *The Glorious Cause: The American Revolution, 1763–1789* (New York: Oxford University Press, Inc., 2005), pp. 290–291. From THE GLORIOUS CAUSE: THE AMERICAN REVOLUTION, 1763–1789 by Robert Middlekauff, copyright © 2005 by Oxford University Press, Inc. Used by permission of Oxford University Press, Inc.

3. W.J. Wood, *Battles of the Revolutionary War, 1775–1781* (New York: Da Capo Press, 1995), p. 32.

4. Christopher Hibbert, *Redcoats and Rebels: The American Revolution Through British Eyes* (New York: W.W. Norton & Co., 1990), p. 90.

5. Middlekauff, p. 331. From THE GLORIOUS CAUSE: THE AMERICAN REVOLUTION, 1763–1789 by Robert Middlekauff, copyright © 2005 by Oxford University Press, Inc. Used by permission of Oxford University Press, Inc.

6. Daniel Marston, *The American Revolution 1774–1783* (Oxford, U.K.: Osprey Publishing, 2002), p. 42.

7. Wood, p. 149.

8. Ibid., p. 226.

Chapter 3. The Soldiers Speak

1. Joseph Plumb Martin, *A Narrative of a Revolutionary Soldier: Some of the Adventures, Dangers, and Sufferings of Joseph Plumb Martin* (New York: Penguin, 2001), p. 18.

2. Ibid., pp. 22–25.

3. Richard M. Dorson, ed., *Patriots of the American Revolution: True Accounts by Great Americans From Ethan Allen to George Rogers Clark* (New York: Gramercy Books, 1998), pp. 124–126.

4. Hugh F. Rankin, *The American Revolution* (New York: G.P. Putnam's Sons, 1964), p. 179.

5. Christopher Hibbert, *Redcoats and Rebels: The American Revolution Through British Eyes* (New York: W.W. Norton & Co., 1990), pp. 160–161.

6. Ray Raphael, *A People's History of the American Revolution: How Common People Shaped the Fight for Independence* (New York: The New Press, 2001), p. 80.

7. C.A. Jellison, *Ethan Allen: Frontier Rebel* (Syracuse, N.Y.: Syracuse University Press, 1983), p. 137.

8. Raphael, p. 197.

9. Hillsdale College History Department, "Comments on Hessian Troops: Lieutenant W. Hale, Philadelphia, 23 March 1778," <http://www.hillsdale.edu/personal/stewart/war/America/Rev/1778-Hessians.htm> (September 30, 2005).

10. John C. Dann, ed., *The Revolution Remembered: Eyewitness Accounts of the War for Independence*

(Chicago: The University of Chicago Press, 1980), pp. 156–157.

11. Alfred W. Blumrosen and Ruth G. Blumrosen, *Slave Nation: How Slavery United the Colonies & Sparked the American Revolution* (Naperville, Ill.: Sourcebooks, 2005), p. 122.

12. Digital History, "Virginia Assembly's Response, December 14, 1775," n.d., <http://www.digitalhistory.uh.edu/learning_history/revolution/virginia_assembly.cfm> (October 3, 2005).

13. Rhys Isaac, *Landon Carter's Uneasy Kingdom: Revolution and Rebellion on a Virginia Plantation* (New York: Oxford University Press, 2006), pp. 3–4. From LANDON CARTER'S UNEASY KINGDOM: REVOLUTION AND REBELLION ON A VIRGINIA PLANTATION by Rhys Isaac, copyright © Oxford University Press, Inc. 2006. Used by permission of Oxford University Press, Inc.

14. Ibid., pp. 12–13. From LANDON CARTER'S UNEASY KINGDOM: REVOLUTION AND REBELLION ON A VIRGINIA PLANTATION by Rhys Isaac, copyright © Oxford University Press, Inc. 2006. Used by permission of Oxford University Press, Inc.

15. Raphael, p. 263.

Chapter 4. News of the Battles

1. David F. Burg, *The American Revolution: An Eyewitness History* (New York: Facts on File, 2001), p. 93.

2. W.J. Wood, *Battles of the Revolutionary War, 1775–1781* (New York: Da Capo Press, 1995), p. 5.

3. Ray Raphael, *A People's History of the American Revolution: How Common People Shaped the Fight for Independence* (New York: The New Press, 2001), p. 282.

4. Ibid.

5. Ibid., p. 283.

6. Joseph Plumb Martin, *A Narrative of a Revolutionary Soldier: Some of the Adventures, Dangers, and Sufferings of Joseph Plumb Martin* (New York: Penguin, 2001), p. 42.

7. Christopher Hibbert, *Redcoats and Rebels: The American Revolution Through British Eyes* (New York: W.W. Norton & Co., 1990), pp. 150–151.

8. John Glover, "To Jonathan Glover and Azor Orne," in *The American Revolution: Writings From the War of Independence* (New York: The Library of America, 2001), pp. 349–350.

9. Martin, p. 88.

10. Albigence Waldo, "Diary, December 11–29, 1777," in *The American Revolution: Writings From the War of Independence,* pp. 401–402.

11. Hugh F. Rankin, *The American Revolution* (New York: G.P. Putnam's Sons, 1964), p. 261.

12. James Thatcher, *A Military Journal During the Revolutionary War* in Charles E. Hatch, Jr., and Thomas M. Pitkin, eds., *Yorktown: Climax of the Revolution* (Washington, D.C.: National Park Service Source Book I, 1941) <http://www.cr.nps.gov/history/online _books/source/sb1/sb1h.htm> (February 18, 2006).

13. Joseph Plumb Martin, *A Narrative of Some of the Adventures, Dangers and Sufferings of a Revolutionary Soldier; Interspersed with Anecdotes of Incidents That Occurred Within His Own Observation* (Hallowell, Me.: Glazier, Masters & Co., 1830), pp. 165–175, <http:// historymatters.gmu.edu/d/6597/> (February 19, 2006).

14. Hibbert, p. 328.

Chapter 5. The Women of the Revolutionary War

1. Carol Berkin, *Revolutionary Mothers: Women in the Struggle for America's Independence* (New York: Alfred A. Knopf, 2005), p. xi.

2. Robert E. Spiller and Harold Blodgett, eds., *The Roots of National Culture: American Literature to 1830* (New York: The Macmillan Company, 1949), pp. 329–330.

3. Mary Beth Norton, *Liberty's Daughters: The Revolutionary Experience of American Women, 1750–1800* (Boston: Little, Brown and Company, 1980), p. 45.

4. Ray Raphael, *A People's History of the American Revolution: How Common People Shaped the Fight for Independence* (New York: The New Press, 2001), pp. 141–142.

5. Ibid.

6. Women of the American Revolution, "Eliza Wilkinson," n.d., <http://www.americanrevolution.org/women20.html> (September 30, 2005).

7. Norton, pp. 188–189.

Chapter 6. The War in Song and Poetry

1. The Library of Congress, American Memory, "Today in History: April 19, Lexington and Concord," n.d., <http://memory.loc.gov/ammem/today/apr19.html> (January 26, 2005).

2. David F. Burg, *The American Revolution: An Eyewitness History* (New York: Facts on File, 2001), pp. 359–360.

3. Digital History, "The Rebels, 1778," n.d., <http://www.digitalhistory.uh.edu/learning_history/revolution/rebels.cfm> (January 26, 2006).

4. Contemplator.com, "The Dying Redcoat," n.d., <http://www.contemplator.com/america/redcoat.html> (October 5, 2005).

5. Contemplator.com, "The Rich Lady Over the Sea," n.d., <http://www.contemplator.com/america/richlady.html> (October 5, 2005).

6. The James Madison Center, James Madison University, Phillis Wheatley Poems, "Letter and Poem to General Washington," n.d., <http://www.jmu.edu/madison/center/main_pages/madison_archives/era/african/free/wheatley/poems/wash.htm> (January 26, 2006).

7. Ibid.

Chapter 7. "The World Turned Upside Down"

1. The Official Web site of the British Monarchy, Historic Royal Speeches and Writings, George III, "Letter on the Loss of America, Written in the 1780s," <http://www.royal.gov.uk/files/pdf/georgeiii.pdf> (February 4, 2006).

2. "A New York Loyalist to Lord Hardwicke," in *The American Revolution: Writings From the War of Independence* (New York: The Library of America, 2001), p. 790.

3. Ray Raphael, *A People's History of the American Revolution: How Common People Shaped the Fight for Independence* (New York: The New Press, 2001), pp. 176–177.

4. George Washington, "Address to Congress on Resigning Commission," in *George Washington: Writings* (New York: The Library of America, 1997), p. 548.

5. James McHenry, "To Margaret Caldwell," in *The American Revolution: Writings From the War of Independence,* p. 796.

6. Ibid., p. 797.

Further Reading

Allen, Thomas B. *George Washington, Spymaster: How America Outspied the British and Won the Revolutionary War.* Washington, D.C.: National Geographic, 2004.

Anderson, Dale. *Leaders of the American Revolution.* Milwaukee: World Almanac Library, 2005.

Bellar, Susan Provost. *The Revolutionary War.* New York: Benchmark Books, 2003.

Bober, Natalie S. *Countdown to Independence: A Revolution of Ideas in England and Her American Colonies: 1760–1776.* New York: Atheneum Books for Young Readers, 2001.

Martin, Joseph Plumb. Edited by Connie Roop and Peter Roop. *The Diary of Joseph Plumb Martin, a Revolutionary War Soldier.* New York: Benchmark Books, 2001.

McGowen, Tom. *The Revolutionary War and George Washington's Army in American History.* Berkeley Heights, N.J.: Enslow Publishers, Inc., 2004.

Nardo, Don. *Weapons of War.* San Diego: Lucent Books, 2003.

Redmond, Shirley Raye. *Patriots in Petticoats: Heroines of the American Revolution.* New York: Random House, 2004.

Schanzer, Rosalyn. *George vs. George: The Revolutionary War as Seen From Both Sides.* Washington, D.C.: National Geographic, 2004.

Schomp, Virginia. *The Revolutionary War.* New York: Benchmark Books, 2004.

Todd, Anne. *The Revolutionary War.* Mankato, Minn.: Capstone Books, 2001.